THE ANCIENT WAY OF THE SOLAR WARRIOR

ATLANTEAN TEMPLE WISDOM

BY

MICHAEL E. MORGAN

The Ancient Way of the Solar warior

Atlantean Temple Wisdom

This work is dedicated to my Master and Spirit Guide
Yokar, The Last Atlantean

Copyright © 2022 by Michael E. Morgan

All rights reserved. No part of this book may be reproduced
or transmitted in any form or by any means now known or to be
invented, electronic or mechanical, including photocopying,
recording, or by any information storage and retrieval system
without written permission from the author or publisher, except
for the inclusion of brief quotations in a review.

For information write to:
Dawntrader Books, LLC
P.O. Box 621
Wilton, Connecticut
06897
If you are unable to order this book from your
local bookseller, or Amazon.com, you may order
directly from the publisher.
Quantity discounts for organizations are available.

Cover and book design by
Michael E. Morgan
Edited by Joe Pierson

Publisher's Cataloging-in-Publication Data
ISBN 978-1732-298-132
10 9 8 7 6 5 4 3 2

Table of Contents

Introduction..4
Chapter 1. Temple Attire...15
Chapter 2. Supplements and Food................................19
Chapter 3. Gathering Agogik Power.............................24
Chapter 4. An Alter, Repetition and Resonance...........27
Chapter 5. Concentration, Imagination, The Sphere....31
Chapter 6. Natural Light, Use of the Sun.....................37
Chapter 7. Use of the Prism..42
Chapter 8. Time Control,The Taulec Arc.....................49
Chapter 9. The Great Wheel, Gathering Magogik Power............57
Chapter 10. The Puukas..79
Chapter 11. The Hand Mudras......................................87
Chapter 12. Quaternary Placement, First octave..........98
Chapter 13 The Minor Circle, The Buuor Shai...........103
Chapter 14. Rengshalaat, The Animal Forms.............106
Chapter 15. Rengmiatralaat, Sitting meditation..........115
Chapter 16. The Torax, Geometric Emotional Cleansing...........126
Chapter 17. The Dragon's Breath................................144
Chapter 18. Sound Power, Mantras.............................153
Chapter 19. Fourths, Fifths, The Anneagram..............160.
Chapter 20. Other Dimensions,The Quantum............166
Chapter 21. Astral Travel..170
Chapter 22. Remote Viewing......................................175
Chapter 23. Lucid Dream Control...............................179
Chapter 24. The Plasma Ball, Signs of Progress........187
Epilogue..192
Tools needed for the work..193

Introduction

This information I obtained from my out-of-body journeys in time to the continent of Atlantis. At the time, I did not have a sense of the coordination or sequence. So, the information was somewhat fragmented, confusing, and difficult to understand.

Most of the information was taken from my master's diary. He left this diary behind before he ascended. His hope was, I would succeed and find it in a hiding place within his last domicile, a cave at the top of Mount Polinar.

Over the years, I have looked back and reviewed the material and begun to reorder the sequence of the training, to put all of it into proper perspective. It is intended to be practiced in the light of one's own circumstances in life, whether those circumstances are supportive or not.

The "work" as described is not a linear system that one might expect upon engaging with this manual. Actually, it is designed to comprise one's own journey or process as one attempts to apply the principles into daily life.

The feelings that arise with both the advocacy of doing the work, as well as the feelings that arise when one does not or cannot do the work, are equally important to the overall view of the real work at hand.

This is the study of the development of the individual's value and the change of one's own perspective of one's own value, as the work implies. The training represents a complete system that can and will alter one's own sense of value, which evolves continuously into higher levels of being and further on to the Quantum.

The aspirant may be concerned with the seemingly voluminous level of time required to accomplish all that is set herein. I hasten to add, further understanding of the synchronistic and harmonistic laws that apply should be reviewed and understood.

The precise pattern of the practices as performed is completely up to the individual and their own discernment based upon their own experiences. This manual is intended as a detailed guideline to follow. The system is designed to be integrated into one's life, not as an adjunct to one's life. Only in this way can one begin to digest the effects of what is developed later.

To begin with, the energy level in the average human being is far below that which is required to maintain a truly healthy existence. The effect of low or poor energy levels defines what is called aging (a form of disease) and illness. Now the average lifespan of a human is between seventy and one hundred years. It is believed by some scientists if a human cell is given adequate nutrition and a pure environment, the probability that the cell will live a thousand years is confirmed. The lifespan, genetically speaking, was originally one thousand years. Canon texts have described Methuselah and others to have lived close to that span of life.

Since the arrival of the Annunaki species, the human span is genetically reduced. The idea of a longer life is not meant to suggest that one needs a thousand years in which to master the system. The effort is not directly proportional to the result desired. In other words, the relative success with the system is dependent on the degree one can allow changes to occur within the body and soul, as well as digest those changes after they have been set into motion.

Much of the work in the system is based upon one's own ability to adapt to the changes quickly. This will vary from one individual to another. Do not consider the ability or lack thereof to render adequate digestion of the energy and the changes it brings as a way to measure your success with the system, compared with another. Remember, the aspirant is the only authority as regards their development. It is just as important to recognize one's resistance. The practitioner must be able to sustain a compassionate attitude toward their own lack of passion for the work from time to time. If that feeling emerges, they must realize they are in a state of indigestion.

Introduction

The individual should try to find their own natural rhythm in applying the work in their own life. Their life is the benchmark in this case. If they squeeze themselves into the work and make their life conform by force, they are already creating more effort against themselves in the long run. Always approach the work with a sense of joy around it.

A set pattern of time and place is very helpful and invokes the rule of harmonic convergence, which multiplies the efforts over time. If the time arises that the individual is not motivated to do the work, then they should accept it as a time for digestion, spending the relaxing time reviewing their feelings while resting. If feelings should arise of guilt and/or worry that the practice is not done enough, then try to realize that it reveals intolerance for the growth and the changes happening.

The diary mentions something called ignition. It is necessary and should be sought after before much of the work can be accomplished. Ignition refers to a threshold whereby an internal chain reaction begins. Imagine a room full of
ping-pong balls loaded into mousetraps, spring loaded to release. If a few individual balls are released into the room, they will strike some of the loaded balls, releasing them. Those will land on other balls, and in turn release them until

the whole room is releasing all of the bound balls. Metaphorically, the energy network within the cells called mitochondria are like this example.

This trigger energy must be had from the life force that surrounds us, not the small reserve that exists within the lower back, which is referred to as the life battery, present to save the life of the individual only in an extreme case. The practitioner will soon see that some of the exercises are designed to build enormous amounts of life force within the cells. This resource can then be used to perform the work, once triggered and stabilized within the body and managed in everyday activities. Though the system utilizes the life force in the form of sexual energy, the practice does not require the individual to abstain or become celibate.

The diary suggests that the Nine Levels of the Dragon's Breath is the practice that encourages ignition. The Dragon's Breath is not a prerequisite to ignition but can help to promote the possibility to occur. Specifically, ignition is a matter of vibration. Ignition occurs when all the cells composing the mitochondria network begin to vibrate synchronistically, meaning they all vibrate at the same frequency. This is called singularity.

All the practices begin to train the body to respond to windows of energetic opportunity automatically. This effect brings the body-mind-soul into complete natural balance with nature. This way is the evolutionary way man was intended to be from the beginning. Then, this frees the soul of man to enter the Quantum, leaving the field of the physical at will and engaging with all levels of reality.

In this spiritual system, some basic concepts regarding its application need to be reviewed. In the Atlantean approach, natural forces at play in the earth environment are included in order to understand the basic principles of the practice.

There are three primary forces hidden within the Prime Mover: Agogik, the (male) positive force, Magogik, the (female) negative force, and Peruitii Rogalin, the neutralizing force.

These three forces are primary in the understanding of working with the Prime Mover externally and internally in the Atlantean spiritual system. First, it is important to understand the concept of the soul. The modern belief is distorted. It is incorrect to assume that souls exist for everyone automatically. A soul only comes into being when a sufficient number of positive higher experiences arise through an increase in understanding from many incarnations.

Only when the understanding begins to increase and the

individual experiences an urge to question and to seek greater understanding does the appearance of the soul emerge. Before this, any approach to real spiritual work becomes moot.

There are some specific points to take into consideration. There are two primary directions that consciousness can take: what might be perceived as an upward direction or creative movement and a downward direction or procreative movement. The downward direction would be best described as populating the earth, whereas the upward direction is turning away from that purpose and developing a higher purpose, to expand and evolve the realm of the prime mover or Quantum.

For the sake of focus, the Prime Mover is called the Most High. Here, the concept of God is also a distortion. The influence of religious belief on the spiritually ignorant creates the predilection to seek something anthropomorphic representing a physical/spiritual entity higher than the individual. The true concept is that the Most High or Prime Mover is really "the way" of all life, a natural evolution in the physical universe, as well as the other dimensions of existence.

There are three aspects of consciousness in the human form. First, there is the body, a separate consciousness that forms the overriding control of bodily functions relegated to the sympathetic and parasympathetic nerve networks.

The sympathetic governs physical conscious actions such as walking, talking, eating, etc. The parasympathetic nerve network controls the automatic life-sustaining actions such as digestion, heart, lungs, and endocrine secretions.

On the level of mind, there are three elements. There is the so-called conscious mind, which includes thought, imagination and reason. Then there is the unconscious mind, which is not recognizable and basically unreachable by ordinary actions. It represents the hind brain or reptilian brain that functions by virtue of instinct. Finally, there is the supra mind, which only arises when there is the emergence of the soul.

Here, we must consider our genetic history as Homo sapiens sapiens. During the prediluvian era, alien species came to the Earth and tampered with the existing bipedal creatures known as the Neanderthal and Cro-Magnon, very early versions of humans.

The Cro-Magnon version arose from the first DNA interference by the Annunaki alien species arriving here around 450,000 BC, made possible by DNA modification. The ultimate result was the final model called the Homo sapiens sapiens.

The natural evolution of man's progression was interrupted. The lifespan was shortened from a thousand years to a hundred years. The forebrain was introduced, to allow for more intelligence for complicated activity with complicated instrumentalities. More importantly, the ability to evolve to a higher level of consciousness is also partially inhibited by the addition of the amygdala, added to the hindbrain as a stopgap to higher evolutionary function.

There is a set of endocrine glands that operate separately. They are governed by the parasympathetic nervous network. They function within the body as ductless glands, secreting hormones and enzymes into the system directly to control body features such as height, body shape, and mental acuity from birth. The hormones also control the biological function of procreation and digestion.

The endocrine system is a basic system established to regulate the normal physical function of the human. When the soul emerges, the development of the supra mind emerges. The possibility exists for the endocrine system to evolve and produce a whole new set of hormones (unknown to present science) that relate to and support higher spiritual function.

This evolution only develops when the individual begins to operate with the intention to cease the downward movement in favor of the upward movement and only when specific spiritual practices are applied, such as with this system.

This system, Tel Shai Ya, is called the Solar system because it is a system based on fire. The other original systems that arose from Lemuria are based upon the element of water. Most of the spiritual descendant systems reflecting that approach exist in some form in Asia today.

The result of a water-based system is limited due to the inherent limitation that the energy of water can only increase the feminine aspect or mental functioning, and there is insufficient energy to affect the other important aspects of positive male development, in short, this leads to the mental body development only and not beyond.

There are seven energy centers existing within the human body. These energy centers are not point sources (as with the Indo-Aryan system) but considered as windows of perception called Puukas, representing seven different aspects of the soul's dimensions. The work with the Puukas is to balance them with the three elements of the Prime Mover, meaning positive, negative, and neutralizing components. The spiritual practices in this system apply these principles to the Puukas.

The elements of light in the form of colors are also used

in this system from a natural source such as the sun through the use of prisms developing the seven aspects of the seven Puukas representing natural food to nurture the "light body" that develops, comprising the higher vibrational functioning of the soul.

Sound is also used to create the vibrational shape necessary to actualize the modification and correct alignment to the Prime Mover, also known as the Quantum by today's science.

Externally, the forces of the earth, heaven (upper atmosphere), the star constellations, and the sun are considered in this practice. Considerations for the application of balance, harmony, and resonance are also important factors considered in this practice.

The understanding of timing for the work, emotional cleansing, training of the mind, willpower, and the application of shape and space also play an essential part of the work as it proceeds to completion.

The spiritual language utilized in this work is call Vril. It contains fifty-two sounds that are spoken aloud and twenty sounds that are spoken silently. When speaking vril, it comes mainly from the unnamed organ at the base of the throat. The sounds are audibly silent, spoken with the mind, and the lips are parted slightly to allow the vibrations to exit the body. The sounds have strong consonants and vowels.

Temple Attire

In Atlantis, everyone wore attire specific to their role in society. As in the story of Atlantis, the tribal clans were divided into specific skill sets relevant to their locale and purpose in the community.

The regional governors wore their robes of leadership and authority on the council. Though each was very similar, they differed by what tribe they hailed from. The material combination was cotton and silk as an undergarment reflecting their tribe, with an overlay of bright red and robes of black. A sling of crystalline stones defining their rank draped over one shoulder across the chest.

For example, the Baal tribe were the makers of things needed for everyone in the community, and their attire reflected that purpose. They wore leather tunics over their shirt jackets with matching pants, and their color was a dark blue that was made of a spun cotton and silk.

The Yaga tribe were the builders and architects. They wore a tunic of leather, and their shirt jacket and pants were also made of a spun cotton and silk, but the color was a dark burnt orange. The Faeylan tribe were the hunters and fishermen. They wore a leather tunic over their shirt jacket and pants to match, also made of spun cotton and silk, with their color a pale forest green. The Saliene tribe were the farmers. also wearing a leather tunic over their shirt jacket with pants to match, made with the same material of spun cotton and silk, and their color was a pale yellow.

The Tasher tribe were the priesthood and gazers. They wore the leather tunic over their shirt jacket and pants to match, made of spun cotton and silk with the color of pale purple. Attached from behind draped a long cape of darker purple with a medallion hung about their neck and shoulders clasped with gold and a crystal of Ariculum as a centerpiece reflecting their ordained rank.

Finally, the Togal tribe were the warriors. They wore leather tunics as well. Their shirt jackets and pants were also made of the same spun cotton and silk. Their color was pure white. Their leather tunics were bound together by a set of crossover loops and pins coupled in back by a short cape attached in cross-draped fashion, similar to ancient Roman military attire. Embedded on the tunic was a breastplate made of stainless steel, bearing the emblem of the realm, a double-headed full-wing spread of the Cahwyll.

In addition, the tunic also covered the shoulders with stainless-steel shoulder cups. The forearms, calves and shins were also covered with leather sheaths embedded with the stainless metal for protection in battle.

Those of the neophyte aspirants still in temple training, ascribing to temple life and devoted to the way of natural forces, differed from the ordained priesthood attire described before. They wore the basic silk and cotton garments of light-purple color only.

The modern-day aspirant seeking greater understanding of the natural forces and ascribing to the sole purpose of spiritual consciousness and enlightenment needs to be conscious of the importance of proper attire for the work.

When donning the attire before beginning your daily focus on the spiritual work, the attire prepares the mind to consciously separate the daily activities of life in the modern world from the activities and focus of the higher realms.

Perhaps it could also be said of changing the attire for going to work in the business world, regardless of the task required, compared to the casual attire while at home. More importantly, the unique properties of the material worn are specifically called for in this case.

Much of the clothing worn in the modern world is made of artificial materials such as Dacron or polyester. These materials are made by an electrochemical process. The fashion of these materials easily yields very colorful patterns suitable to fashionable taste but very detrimental to the human organic processes.

Polyester is a synthetic fiber created from coal and petroleum. Rayon is a semi-synthetic fiber made from reconstituted wood pulp. Spandex, also known as Lycra or Elastane, is a synthetic fiber characterized by its extreme elasticity. All of these involve an embedded electrical property woven into the molecular structure and leave behind a mild electrical field that surrounds the body. It is quite possible that people who wear these garments complain of headaches and/or fatigue and do not realize the effects on the body, such as nervous disorders over a short time. It is not recommended that these be worn at all, even for ordinary life, let alone for spiritual work. It is preferable that real cotton, a cotton-silk combination, and/or linen be worn for the work.

Ideally, if one can find these materials in a pale-purple color, it is very sympathetic and resonant to the upper ranges of vibration supportive to reaching those modes of consciousness. The garments should be loose-fitting as well.

Supplements and Food

The consumption of food is an essential consideration to the spiritual aspirant. In the United States, food products have succumbed to the wiles of manufacturing and business considerations for greater profits, offering improved shelf life and longer survival during the shipping and distribution of food produce.

Insect infestation and crop destruction is also compensated for in the problem of growing more food to supply greater needs of all sorts of foods. The introduction of pesticides to thwart insect infestation, though in principle a good idea, is now a normal activity that is introduced during the growth cycle of crops. Unfortunately, these very toxic compounds to these vermin also end up as an additional component of consumption on the dinner table.

Artificial enzymes and hormone additives chemically produced and added to feed for poultry and beef are designed to make the beef or chickens fatter and healthier but cannot be removed during the processing and end up adversely affecting human hormone balance and creating various forms of hidden disease to humans, shortening their lifespan.

In recent times, cattle and chicken ranchers looking to reduce the cost of feed make better use of otherwise lost or wasted animals who have died because of disease or other causes. They have taken to grinding up the remains of these dead animals and adding it back into the feed to the living produce, thus increasing their feed supply and reducing their costs. The unregulated food industry led to the unforeseen effects of this behavior, erupting in disastrous effects for human consumption, such as mad cow disease.

Chicken, like beef, is a major staple of the food-supply industry. Feeding chickens with these hormones and holding them in small cages to prevent unnecessary running around causes them to grow bigger and faster, with more fat content, which increases their bottom line based upon their weight at the market.

These hormones end up in the meat and are consumed by children, which offers rapid and unhealthy hormonal changes, creating the unnatural emergence into puberty noted by some science researchers.

Even food produce has been irradiated by nuclear isotopes to prevent early spoilage but can leave radioactive elements to enter the human body, which can cause free radicals to form inside the body and are suspected to cause certain kinds of cancer.

Natural or organic foods have a shortened to-ripe life before they spoil and become unsustainable for long-term shelf life. In recent years, GMO foods are prevalent. Because consciousness is increasing about the dangers of GMO foods and hormones added to foods, there is a sharp rise with farmers offering organic foods. They are more expensive and out of reach financially to many people.

GMO foods have been genetically modified, meaning their properties have been altered at the seed-germination level. This is because whole or natural foods will provide an abundant replenishment with seed replication. An ear of corn, for example, bears more than a hundred seeds from the planting of only one seed. Apples and other fruit contain numerous seeds within the pulp, and one seed will grow into a tree bearing many apples, cherries, or on vines, such as grapes, etc. This is nature's way of ensuring that an abundance of food is propagated.

The business of food growing and manufacturing has succumbed to greed and malice with GMO processes. First, the GMO foods do not have seeds held within their contents, allowing seed sales to be controlled by forcing farmers to grow only the seeds made in this way, disallowing them to create their own continuous seed bank.

It is recommended that a spiritual aspirant consume only natural or organic food if possible. As the saying goes, "you are what you eat." Subtle human energies thrive and function by sunlight. Foods that receive the most direct sunlight are desirable, meaning foods grown above ground. Meats such as beef and chicken are sources of indirect sunlight because the animal eats grains grown in the sunlight, but through their digestion process prevent direct access to the light, causing human consumption much more effort to get the same amount of light.

One does not have to be a strict vegan to support a spiritual path. Actually, it is not recommended, because long-term lack of animal fat will cause the body to draw on needed existing oils within the body. Only a few years need go by before the body will begin to show signs of skin deterioration such as eczema.

Fish is an excellent source of protein, yet it is desirable to eat only those fish that swim near the surface of fresh or saltwater, closer to the light, like perch or salmon, not bottom feeders such as tuna or catfish, as these are more than likely to contain poisonous substances like mercury or radioactive waste dumped into the ocean. Shellfish are also bottom feeders and should be eaten rarely.

The idea of supplements is also an important consideration for spiritual work. Some basic principles apply, such as vitamin C with a dosage of 2,000 to 3,000 mg daily will keep the immune system high. Source Naturals offers 1,500-mg dosage in one tablet with rosehips. A good multivitamin is recommended as well.

Specific supplements are also recommended to feed the endocrine system, such as Red Korean Ginseng in liquid form and Royal Jelly also in liquid form. Prince of Peace makes a good combination in a small vial, with thirty vials to a package.

Begin this supplement slowly as half a bottle every other day for a week, to see if there is any adverse reaction to the royal jelly supplement. This supplement directly supports all of the endocrine glands and keeps them vibrant and healthy and provides much-needed energy for the work. Resveratrol, called Nitro250 capsules, is excellent and available from Revgenetics taken along with NMN daily are together fortifying for the body and promote anti-aging. Fresh water should be consumed daily, as internal heat will be generated with the work causing potential dehydration. So, thirty-two ounces daily is recommended.

Gathering Agogik Power

In the Atlantean Temple, concepts of energy were presented as two elements that are considered. First, there is the Earth Dragon, a great source of Agogik energy, and second, there is the Sky Dragon, a great source of Magogik energy. When these two energies are gathered sufficiently within the body, the third force, Perutii Rogalin, the neutral force, arises. This force is the balancing force that stimulates the creation of the Light Body.

Surrounding the earth are series of energy lines of earth force also called ley lines. Where they intersect constitutes a point source that can be used to draw power from the earth, also called the Odic force, useful in the first part of the Agogik energy work needed for creating the neutralizing force within the body.

There are some crossing zones where extreme energy vortexes are created. One such location is located beneath the Great Pyramid of Giza in Egypt. In that place, five lines intersect. If you could go to the Great Pyramid and descend to the bottom pit, five hundred feet below the surface, it is the most desirable place to draw Agogik power.

The second location where five lines intersect, along with seven streams of water crossing below the main cathedral floor is the gothic Cathedral Charte in France. There, the Druidic priests created the labyrinth pattern on the floor, walking through the pattern by aspirants of the Druidic practices.

Once the sensitivity is developed in the work, the practitioner will be able to locate places where two or three lines intersect that are quite effective. One place is in California, called Giant Rock. There, three lines intersect below the huge crystalline quartz stone. Famously made known by the scientist George Van Tassel where, in the late sixties, George gathered UFO enthusiasts before he died. There are many places where two lines cross, and those are very effective sources of Agogik energy as well, which can be stored in the body for the work to proceed.

These energy zones where the lines converge and pool their energy is not automatically offered to the casual passerby. Secret techniques need to be used to draw up the power into the body. That technique to be used is presented later on in this manual.

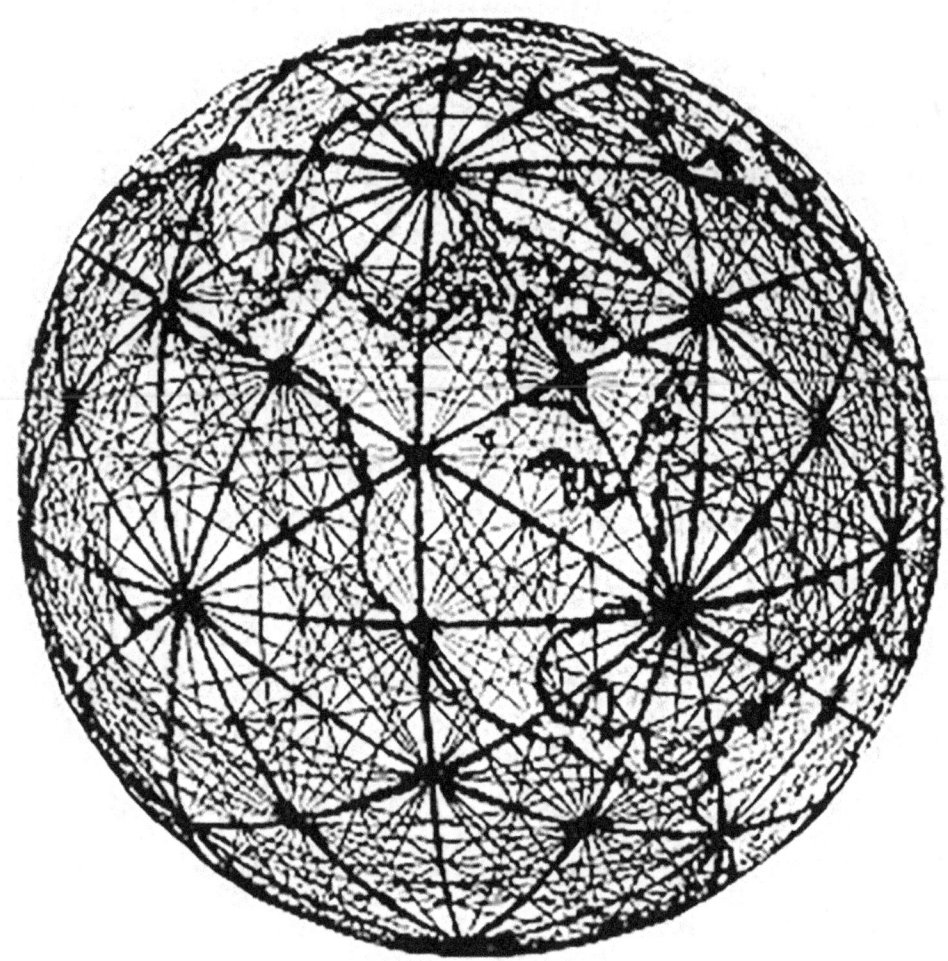

The Earth Grid or ley line Grid, the Earth Dragon's Path

The Grid Illustration #1

An Alter, Resonance in Repetition

The most common meaning of the term an altar represents a votive location where one can come and offer prayers for some request to a deity respective to a specific religious belief. Here, the concept is not so specific but determines a unique place where the spiritual work and subsequent devotional attitude can be exercised.

The idea of repetitive action is generally accepted with performing some sort of development work, such as physical exercise with a goal of physical health and strength. With this action some location is determined, such as a gym or place where workout gear is situated. In this case, the idea is expanded to mental, emotional, psychological, and physical actions combined related to the goal of spiritual strength and development.

In the religious sense, there is imposed an obligation to return to a place of worship regularly, such as going to church on a Sunday ad infinitum, with an assured promise that doing so will assure the individual a place in heaven in the afterlife (a major misconception).

The original importance of using a similar day and time is cloaked. The sense of obligation to do so is steeped in guilt and fear, as well as judgment socially among the other followers of a similar belief system. This constitutes strong peer pressure to comply (another misconception).

In the Atlantean spiritual work, any obligation imposed is by and to oneself, not due to any peer pressure or an obligation to a community or social group. This positive attitude is absolutely critical to ultimate success. A sense of complete honesty with oneself is expected, meaning that if the desire is not present, then one does not do the work. Only when the joy, self-confidence, and eagerness to do the work is present will success with the work be assured. Otherwise, if the self (the mind, body, and emotions) is not aligned behind any action, it is holding back with the life stream or force. The general rule here is: if one holds back on one thing or area, then all is held back, and no progress can be obtained.

Getting back to repetition, it supplies two aspects. First it is generally understood that repetition means practice in an action until a level of mastery is acquired. The second part of repetition respects to something called resonance.
An example of resonance is:

If a wave of energy strikes against a glass and that wave happens to be vibrating at a frequency that is similar to the inherent resonant frequency of the glass, the energy of the vibration will cause the glass to vibrate in synchrony. The two vibrations will add together causing the integrity of the glass to eventually break. This happens because the vibrations of the glass and the vibration of the oncoming vibration add together and will increase in amplitude or intensity until the glass losses its integrity and shatters.

This means that the increase of strength of an action, be it physical, mental, emotional, or psychological, or all of these combined with such force applied and with a similar frequency that is similar or equal to and close to the original action called "the natural frequency" of the system of action, will in time increase in strength (amplitude) as opposed to a similar action done at a nonresonant time.
Nonresonant actions operate independently in time and space and do not connect easily.

So, with this idea in mind, one needs to approach the work always at the same day and same time, each time. The law follows that the increase in the resonant action will multiply by virtue that there is a symbiotic (quantum) connection through time and space of all the resonant actions, thus causing the increase of strength through the multiplication of all those experiences summed in time and space.

The secondary benefit unseen by the practitioner is the effect of resonance upon the elemental components of an environment. The underpinning idea is that all matter is conscious in one degree or another. With this said, the environment will become tuned to the repetitive actions and begin to resonate with the actions.

    The elementals seeking continued experience of the action will attempt to gather all elements together, including the one who began the experience, meaning the practitioner. In short, if the practitioner continues in a resonant way, the environment will call to the practitioner when the time grows near to resonance.

Concentration, Imagination, the Ball

Most people will experience flashes of images of many things over time. Few people could not sustain any image or part of an image for more than a few seconds. The most experienced sort of people may be able to hold an image for as long as five minutes or more.

Some of the many tools a seeker may conjure and need in order to further the work will also possess some of the tools not physical, such as the power to imagine and sustain the imagined thing for at least fifteen minutes. When that is accomplished, it is said this skill has been attained.

It's one thing to say an image is present, but to what degree, meaning is the image clear and readily available for definitions which could only arise with the second property that is an equally important tool: the power to concentrate? To mentally control the focus of your attention that is illuminating your mind, until the most insignificant property of a thing is noticed equally.

As powerful as each ability is, in their respect to the overall total capacity of a human being's consciousness, they would both be enhanced greatly in their joining in with a common effort. When the imagination is armed with concentration, there is no comparison to the level and amplitude of that powerful combination, and then one is capable of just about anything.

The strengthening exercises in this part will seem insignificant and perhaps a waste of time (though no one can actually waste time). In time, however, a degree of patience coming from the self offers the seeker a significant advantage in accelerating their progress.

Exercise #1.
Pick an object that is small, perhaps unusual in shape, with any unusual surface characteristics, such as a strong reflective property that casts strong light into the view of the seeker. Then close the eyes and turn the focus inward into the dark. Begin to recall seeing the object. Once having captured the image, continue to hold the image while you fine tune the focus into creating greater detail about the image.

With practice comes progress. So, daily viewing the object for one minute at a time will provide strong possibilities to recreate the image in clearer and greater detail with each successive repetition. Continue with this action until the image can be held for two minutes. Continue for a time at this level before moving on to the fifteen-minute period. Growth in small steps provide the best approach only when this level of mastery is attained. This will establish a solid base of experience to rely on later.

Concentration, Imagination, the Ball

Concentration is not the same as imagination, an element where only freedom of movement is absolute and necessary, whereas concentration requires a steady but focused range of consciousness, steady and calm that begins as a cone-shaped funnel of awareness where at the apex, the thrust of mind falls toward the focal point, at the heart or center of the object. (This is the point of greatest detail.)

Exercise #2.
Begin at the number 100. Close the eyes and begin to count backward to zero. When that has been achieved, then extend the count to a thousand, counting back to zero. Then, close the eyes and focus on the English alphabet letters. Begin to visualize each letter, holding it for five seconds and then recalling its predecessor letter, such as Z-Y- #. Visualize all the letters in reverse position from Z and ending with A.

Exercise #3.
The unusual but simple objects used before provided many cues for your consciousness to begin recalling an image. Now the skill must be increased so that the lack of surface anomalies will not be present to rely on for recall. For this, one needs a small ball, smooth and perfectly round, to help aid the visual process. The ball should be a crystal or acrylic

ball between three-quarters and one inch in diameter.

The aspirant must hold the sphere between the thumb and forefinger at arm's length. Stare at the crystal for ten seconds. Take a breath and close the eyes. Begin to recall what the crystal ball looked like when viewing it with the eyes open in your mind. You must go beyond the flash of the image, whether whole or in part; you must hold the image and do not let go of it, for as long as you can manage. Note the light reflections and any other image reflected from the surface from the nearby surroundings.

When you have successfully visualized the ball without losing it for fifteen minutes, then you must proceed to move the ball around in front of your inside sight without losing it. When you have accomplished this, then change the shape to a cube or pyramid and also choose these shapes with different colors.

Exercise #4.
Purchase a small amount of sculpting clay, clay that will remain soft and not harden over time. This could be purchased at a craft store. Knead the clay until it is easy to mold in the hand. You will close your eyes and keep them closed during this exercise and will not open your eyes until you are finished molding.

First, you are to mold a small, four-sided pyramid. The sides must be even and at the same angle with the edges sharp and defined. The base must be flat. You must repeat this exercise until the shape is nearly perfect.

Second, you must mold a three-sided pyramid following the same parameters as with the four-sided pyramid. Repeat until nearly perfect, and remember, you must keep your eyes closed. If you peek to check your progress, then you must start over with a rounded lump. During this exercise, the benefit is to hold the image the whole time you are molding the shape. Repeat these exercises until the shapes are nearly perfect.

Exercise #5.
Choose a memory of a dwelling that you lived in as a child. You must see it in the mind's eye as clearly as if you were actually looking at it. You must see all of it, not just bits and pieces. Begin to approach your childhood dwelling from the street, far and away, so that you would walk down the street toward it, noting everything around you with as much detail as you can muster. When you arrive at your dwelling, go behind and around the dwelling, noting all details surrounding it.

Now enter the dwelling and go to each room, upstairs

and down if it is a two-story building. Note the kitchen, the living room with the furniture, and the baths and bedroom with its furniture. Note all of the colors of each item, and note any wall hangings such as photographs or paintings complete in detail, including the colors.

Continue with this exercise until you can see it plainly. Then go on to your place of learning, your school. Inside, walk the hallways and any classrooms you frequented. Go to the village or town where your dwelling existed. Continue this exercise until all is perfectly clear without dropping it and with your eyes always closed.

The Ball Illustration #2

Natural Light, Use of Sunlight

Natural light is the light that comes from the sun. This kind of light is considered white light, even though when it is brought through a prism, it divides into the seven-color spectrum of visible light. The sun also emits light in the infrared range, as well as the ultraviolet range, which are outside of the normal range of detection by the human eye.

The advantage of sunlight is it is generated by atomic interactions. Many scientists say the sun generates its light and heat through the process of fusion, but when fusion occurs, there are high-speed particles generated called neutrinos. There are no neutrinos detected coming from the sun. Some scientists have said they don't know why the sun shines. So, we must conclude the sun shines for sure, but exactly how is a mystery.

In these modern days, we have more than one kind of light source. We have moved beyond the use of kerosene lamps to electric incandescent lights invented by Thomas Edison in 1879 in Menlo Park, New Jersey, at his lab. These bulbs are still made and widely in use in homes today. A new kind of solid-state light emits light from a semiconductor junction called a light-emitting diode or LED. These lights do not use AC or alternating current but are DC or direct-current driven.

These lights are far more rugged and last for years

compared to the electric light bulb, which depends on a high-resistive filament and lasts only for several hundred hours. In addition, these LED lights are far less wasteful in the use of power than the traditional incandescent lights and are growing in popularity. Specially adapted incandescent-type light bulbs designed to fit into common electrical sockets have LEDs inside now, made to look like incandescent bulbs.

There is also fluorescent lighting, a tube filled with gas such as argon, xenon, neon, or krypton, and mercury vapor. The pressure inside the lamp is around 0.3 percent of atmospheric pressure. The gas is excited by electrical discharge to illuminate, similar to the flash lamps for strobes. These tubes run continuously and are used in factories and many businesses, providing a cheaper form of efficient light.

Light emitted from a laser is unique because it is not scattered, meaning the light is radiated at a single frequency and does not spread out randomly like an incandescent bulb. When light is coherent, the light is of only one frequency and can be confined to a narrow beam and focused with lenses, which can be so intense it can cut through metal. Laser stands for light amplification by stimulated emission of radiation. The original invention, by Theodore Maimin in

1960 at the Hughes Laboratory consisted of a ruby rod excited by a xenon flash lamp. Now new discoveries have generated lasers that come in all sorts of varieties and colors. Lasers operating in microwave frequencies are called masers. There are also carbon dioxide lasers and solid-state lasers using crystals.

Special lighting used in photography, such as xenon gas flash lamps, are used for strobe technology. The sharp, staccato nature of these short bursts can be used to visually freeze rotating objects for speed tests or for entertainment in discotheques as special effects.

All artificial light, though useful in its own right, is spiritually dead. This means it has no life-giving property other than illuminating dark areas in the environment. Life support is true as far as providing certain safety where malicious intent or crime cannot be carried out except in dark places.

Normally, artificial light should not be used for spiritual work. Certain special cases of LED light are used photonically to stimulate with the application of red light in unique devices designed to supplant improved brain function and altered brain states.

Normal brain function is bifurcated or divided in the two hemispheres, preventing spiritual development. Strobed photonic stimulation can be used to overcome bifurcation function through brainwave synchronization that provides whole-brain function, meaning both hemispheres operating together.

The light from the sun is known for stimulating vitamin D in living organisms such as man. It is the best light for healthy functioning of the endocrine glands too. It has been a resource of lifegiving properties to all living creatures since the dawn of creation and known scientifically as a basic staple of life processes on any planet.

In the early cultures on Earth, the sun was also revered as a god. The Atlantean spiritual system focused on the "light of the one," first utilized in their Taoi stones, large crystals providing light, heat, and power for an energy field that supplied all the transmissive energy for their transport systems. Then later, also as a weapon, called a Mash-Maak, the very first laser.

Later on, the Atlanteans developed the use of sunlight in their healing temples, such as the Temple of Beauty. Then they learned these healing colors could be used for enhancing spiritual development. They used large prisms to divide the white sunlight into its lifegiving specific frequencies (the seven colors) to heal. They developed the use of the colors to provide pure food in the form of specific energy frequencies needed for nurturing the Puukas (an Atlantean term describing the energy centers), composing the energetic structure of the "light body" created through development.

The Use of the Prism

Color is a very important part of spiritual training in the Atlantean spiritual system. It is as important as the food that you consume. The difference is this kind of food is light energy, supplying the nutrients for the growth of the light body.

There are two kinds of light, light that is transmitted and light that is reflected. Though light that is transmitted is the primary focus of this part of the work, it is important to note that light reflected also has an influence on the psyche.

In this case, the colors of a surrounding space such as a room one would use for meditation is significant. By contrast, you would not want a room brightly colored with all sorts of wild patterns intermixed with different colors. This would not be conducive to a meditative state, whereas a room colored with a softer pastel such as a violet or light blue would offer better circumstances to support an inner awakening.

The clothing one wears also can be supportive while doing the work. Note, for example, a doctor or nurse either wears a light green color or white. These are suggestive of growth and healing. On the other hand, those practicing the martial arts often wear black or brown, a color reflecting the use of the shadow energies for combat.

It is interesting to note that reflective colors are actually not the true color of the material but their complement. If you examine a roll of negative film, you will see that the light colors are dark, and the dark colors are light. Specific colors are the complement of the actual colors when printed. Then it is interesting to realize that as you perceive the world around you, it is not what you believe it to be in your perception but its opposite. In many ways, the world around you is but an illusion of what it really is.

When it comes to transmissive color, we must consider the source of that light energy. In this case, it must come from a natural source. That source is the sun.

Like everything else, the sun is also subject to evolution. Many years ago, one could look up into the sky and observe the distinctly yellow hue of the sunlight overhead. Now the sun is a blue-white color, indicating the sun's inner nature has changed to reflect the needs of the solar system and life in it to evolve and change as well. All energy evolves to a higher harmonic naturally. Also, all life evolves to a higher nature and quality.

Though science suggests that the sun is a ball of very hot plasma, like all stars, coming from the decay of hydrogen into helium, the sun is also not what it appears to be. It is, in fact, a portal to a higher dimension, and the light exuding from it reflects that energy which, in its essence, is spiritual, and so the older civilizations peering at the sun knew subconsciously that it was a kind of god or the presence of a higher nature governing all life on the planet.

For this work, the aspirant will need to obtain a crystal prism, made of high-quality optical glass. Though seven colors are divided through the prism diffraction process, only six colors are needed, eliminating infrared.
The shape of the crystal is also important. The shape needs to be similar to a diamond, with eight facets on each side, generally octagonal and somewhat flattened in appearance.

The size of the crystal is about three inches in diameter, easily held in the hand. In the past, Swarovski made such a crystal for some of their lighting fixtures. A similar item can be purchased through Etsy model # f7-014 Prism Paperweight Lead Crystal Faceted with Eight Sides, three inches in diameter. See the illustration on the following page with its proper application.
The prism is held in the hand, usually in the morning, around 10 a.m. The angle of the sun pointed at the prism will emit the colors with a wide enough spread to be useful and convenient.

The colors will be bright and vivid. These colors are brought through the crystal, not as a reflection on the surface. So, the aspirant must adjust the angle of the prism until all of the colors are emitted from the opposite side.

Each color can be singled out for observation with a little practice.

Because pure sunlight is streaming through the prism, the aspirant must not view the colors directly, but off center from the direct view. Note this detail in the illustration as well. Beginning practice should be thirty seconds with each eye, with a maximum exposure of one minute per each color; red, orange, yellow, green, blue, light blue, violet. The pattern of viewing used is to consider the color viewed as the center of an imaginary clock face, where the view is off center by about two to three inches, holding the view in each eye until the view turns dark.

This means that the eye has become overstimulated and cannot take in the energy in that position any longer. So, the aspirant must move to the next position around the imaginary clock: 12-1-2-3-4-5-6-7-8-9-10-11. Each position should last approximately five seconds, maybe less for each individual until complete. Do not view for more than a minute for each color.

The Puukas (windows) are not open to accepting the light of the colors all the time. Some will reject the energy, while others will accept the energy. The aspirant must learn when these opportunities arise with each set of practices. It is suggested this practice be done once per week at firin- creasing to three times as sunlight opportunity permits. Note the sunlight must be a bright and sunny day, with little or no clouds or haziness. Note: The ultraviolet is visible only slightly as a slight purple halo and not direct.

The prism Illustration # 3

The Use of the prism

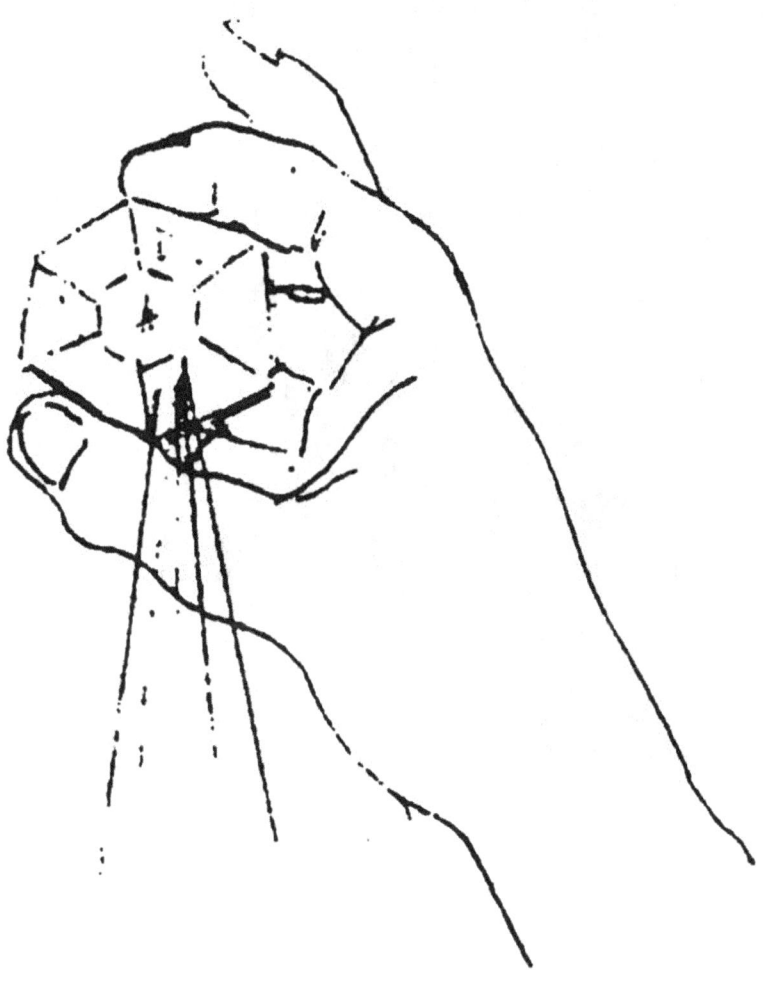

The prism Illustration # 4

48 The Use of the prism

The prism Usage Illustration # 5

Time Control, the Taumlec Arc

In the Atlantean spiritual practice, the issue of time is significant. Very often, philosophers will reflect on time as mercurial, meaning illusory. It is often noted by many that time is somewhat relative. For example, when one makes a journey to another location, it is often sensed to take longer than the return journey. Or when one is preoccupied by an activity, the time seems to shrink, becoming shorter, as compared to doing nothing, where the time expands to a much longer period. As a child, the time would seem almost eternal in a given day, whereas as an adult, time seems to get shorter with age. People often comment that the months and years go by with greater acceleration than when they were younger.

    Spiritually speaking, time is an illusion. There is no time. Masters who have entered into the nether worlds define time to be either relative or nonexistent. Einstein often spoke of the relativity of time and space. Now with the modern concepts of space-time, time can go faster or slower depending on the relationship to light. The idea of bending space and cheating the flow of time offers the idea of practical space travel across vast distances. Where normally it would take light to travel in cartesian space thousands of years to cross, a simple Einstein-Rosen bridge (known as a wormhole) easily short circuits that space and the time to travel the same distance. (In science fiction terms, it is known as warping.) Though now science is on the verge of creating "warp" drives to accomplish just that.

In spiritual terms, altering the mind's view of time has definite benefits. Perception is key in spiritual development. Control of the mind suggests control of space and time at the same time, not unlike the warp drives for space travel. Getting control of time offers the aspirant the possibility of time travel. Moving back and forth in time provides access to greater information useful to the traveler
First, this is a form of advanced clairvoyance and clairaudience. Then at a more advanced form later of this is practice actually moving the body through time, as well as extending the lifespan to unlimited levels even to reach immortality.These properties arise from the practice of the Taumlec Arc.

The Taumlec Arc is a meditational practice requiring perseverance and patience. For the sake of ease, to keep track of the process, a set of beads is utilized. One longer set is made of 240 beads, divided by four individual larger beads with different shapes, and one larger bead has attached a bunch of threads denoting the beginning. Each section defines approximately one minute (or approximately sixty seconds) in each of four directions around a circle or arc and counted mentally in one hand.

A second set of beads, held in the other hand, is shorter in length, with ten sections having a count of nine beads each separated by a larger-sized bead. One larger bead also has fixed with a small bunch of threads attached to define the starting larger bead.

Each set of nine beads represents nine rounds, or one arc. Starting practice must begin with three arcs. This will approximate thirty-six minutes for each arc, for a total of 108 minutes or 1.8 hours.

There are four colors imagined in this practice. A royal-blue color focused at the groin area, followed by a turn of the circle to the right shoulder with the bright green color, then on to the top of the head or crown with a white color, finally back to the left shoulder with a color of bright red. As each color is visualized, the beads of the large string are moved between the thumb and forefinger for sixty beads at each location around the circle. When the unusual-shaped bead is encountered, it's time to move on to the next location around the circle followed with the appropriate color. This is the direction for the male practice.

In the female practice, the blue and white colors remain the same in their positions, but the direction of turn is opposite, meaning from the groin the circle turns first to the left shoulder or red color with the final portion of the circle ending on the right shoulder and green color.

In addition to this, sounds are uttered silently in the mind in each of the four positions around the circle. A set of consonants is spoken silently with each passing bead in the quadrant on the larger bead string. Each consonant set will change at each quadrant of the circle where the full consonant set is uttered silently at each bead passed during that quadrant. See the illustration on the following pages.

The Taumlec Arc is another part of the Lunar (female) alchemy called Rengshalaat, relating to the female fluid energies within the body, such as the seven endocrine hormones and enzymes. It is a fire practice relating to the mind (the female aspect of consciousness). It helps to raise the vibration of the endocrine glands, which aids in psychic development and opens the twelve psychic channels that run along the neck area.

The Vril uttered silently, along with color visualization, also stimulates the psychic fire within the glands, making them sweat (creating fluid) new hormones and enzymes. These promote the evolution of the mind and body while training the mind with focus and concentration and dissolving the influence of empirical time on the consciousness (making the "world" stop and time to slow down and stop). This promotes doing the work within the ticks of the empirical clock. This practice prepares the aspirant for time travel.

In the beginning, the best time to do the Taumlec Arc is in the morning. It's a good way to begin the day. Though it can be done at any time (keeping in mind the importance of choosing the same time and same day—as in the use of harmony and synchrony in its application of effort). After the individual becomes more proficient in the practice, meaning knowing by heart the colors, positions, and Vril at each quadrant of the large bead group, one might prefer to do it at night. The memory peg practice sheet can be done at any time.

1 round of the large bead set = 4 minutes on average
9 rounds of the large bead set = 1 arc = 36 minutes on average

When first beginning this practice, do one arc and do not stop. In general, never stop before completing the nine rounds of the large bead set (thirty-six minutes). Always complete an arc, regardless of how many arcs are done.

With each arc, there is a geometric progression and increase the number by nine rounds of the large bead set (one arc), if the individual feels the urge (feelings) to do more. Do not let the mind determine this increase. So, for example, your first increase would be to do two arcs (one hour and twelve minutes).

Minimum practice will equal nine rounds (one arc) at each sitting. Ultimately, the individual will want to increase to three arcs (one hour and forty-eight minutes) at each sitting. Three arcs are both necessary and recommended for positive results. Gradually increase this meditation time by the influence of the inner-will feelings and not by ambition or the outer-will demand.

It is also recommended to use the ruler after a Taumlec arc meditation, going through the sitting sweep motions and the walking sweep motions.
See the illustration for these movements.

Time Control, the Taumlec Arc

Taumlek Arc meditation

The following practice is done by using the unamed organ as usual. You need to visualize the patterns below and color as I have indicated in the sketch areas.

The Vril sequence and direction of movement for the female is to the left(CCW) and should be done without a focus on the breathing...The Vril sequence and direction of movement for the male is to the right(CW)and should be done without a focus on the breathing. Both movements begin at the perneum. Each position is held with concentrated effort for one (1)minute with a total of four(4) minutes per cycle and repeated for six(6) cycles to equal one arc. A total of 360 arcs should be sought to equal a singular pledge.

The Female Practice:

To begin female sequence: at the base of the spine in the region of the perneum. Begin by visualizing a sphere of deep blue color and hold the position of the eyes downward with some pressure while uttering the Vril: **O.N. J. N. G..**   (O)oh - (N)neh - (J)jed - (N)neh - (G)geh

Next turn the eyes to the left leaving the head stationary, while visualizing an emerald green sphere of intense green light and hold the position of the eyes to the left with some pressure for one minute and then utter the Vril: **K.P.T.H.A.N.**   (K)keh - (P) peh - (T)teh - (H)heh - (A)ah - (N)neh

Next turn the eyes upward toward the crown while visualizing a sphere of intense golden white light and hold the position of the eyes to the top of the head with some pressure for one(1) minute and then utter the Vril: **A. U. M. R. E. T.**   (A)ah - (U)ooh - (M)meh - (R)reh - (E)eh - (T)teh

Next turn the eyes to the right leaving the head stationary while visualizing a sphere of burning bright red fire and hold the position of the eyes to the right with some pressure for one(1) minute and utter the Vril:

R.A.T.R-U.SH-II.   (R)reh - (A)ah - (T)teh - (RU) reh-ooh - (Sh-II) shi - ee

Repeat (4) times for one cycle
Repeat cycle (6)times for one Arc

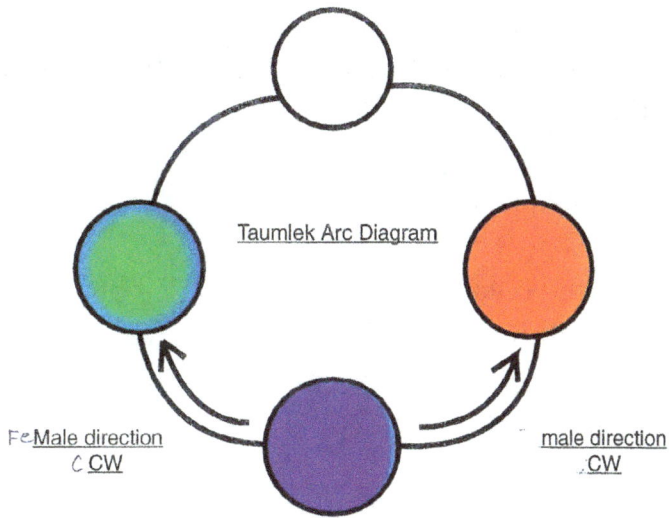

The prism Illustration # 6

Time Control, the Taumlec Arc

Taumlec Arc memory peg practice

1. Sphere = deep blue color , location perineum
   Vril= Oh-Neh-Shed-Neh-Geh
   a. See a deep blue color sphere in the area of the perineum(hold)
   b. Say the Vril out loud
   c. Say the Vril again silently
   d. Say the Vril out loud twice
   e. Say the Vril silently twice
   f. Say the Vril out loud, silently, out loud, silently

2. Sphere=bright green color(male direction) left shoulder location,
   Vril= Keh-Peh-Teh-Heh-Ah-Neh
   a. See the bright green color sphere in the area of the left shoulder (hold)
   b. Say the Vril out loud
   c. Say the Vril again silently
   d. Repeat steps d-f as listed above

3. Sphere=golden white color, location crown
   Vril=Ah-Ooh-Meh-Reh-Eh-Teh
   a. See the bright golden white color sphere at the crown (hold)
   b. Say the Vril out loud
   c. Say the Vril again silently
   d. Repeat steps d-f as listed above

4. Sphere=bright red color(female direction), Right shoulder location,
   Vril= Reh-Ah-Teh-Reh-Ooh-Shi-EE
   a. See the bright Red color sphere, location right shoulder (hold)
   b. Say the Vril out loud
   c. Say the Vril silently
   d. Repeat steps d-f as listed above

Note: The Vril should be said at each bead at perineum. But Vril can be split into half statements on each bead at the shoulders and crown locations.

The Great Wheel, Magogik Power

The same knowledge was derived by the priesthood of Karnak recorded The priests of the Temple of Power were very aware of the sky dragon's power over life on the earth. All activities were governed in Atlantean society, including birth. But birthing time was insignificant and could be random. So, the priests of the Tasher clan, overseers of the Temple of Power, determined that conception was far more important, and procreation was controlled by the conception time of a newborn child, which determined the child's fate and task within the society, casting it into which tribe the child belonged, which in turn was controlled by the energies of the great wheel. Conception time was induced using the knowledge and power of the great wheel and determined by the use of Magik.

Once again, I traveled to the ancient time of the discovery of the great wheel and all of the constellations. Their shape was very different then, some one hundred thousand years ago. I recorded their shapes and reconstructed the wheel as they saw it. I have provided that information in the following illustrations with explanations of each component.

The Atlantean priests developed the knowledge of the Solar Phalanx (the path of the One as it traveled through the great wheel of twenty-six thousand years, the precession of the equinoxes). and sculptured at Dendera (or Denderah) during the eighteenth dynasty (Ca. 1500 BC), a widely known Egyptian bas-relief of the Zodiac from the ceiling of the pronaos (or portico) of a chapel dedicated to Osiris in the Hathor Temple at Dendera, containing images of Taurus (the bull) and Libra (the scales).

The Tasher clan or priest class gave names to each constellation and their meaning and purpose. I recorded those from Yokar's diary here. They also developed a system of astrology based upon 108 stars that offered the most significant influences and used that knowledge for divination purposes.

In the last three thousand years, remnants of this knowledge, though fragmented and incomplete, were used by the Druids (The Druid year of Pleiades).

The witches of the Middle Ages also used a similar form for their own divination. They discovered some aspects of the great wheel that they used to determine the time of Samhein and Beltain as well as Lugnasadh and Embolc for their Wiccan ceremonies.

The astrologer Freidrich Seggrun, utilized by Adolph Hitler, had intuited some of this knowledge through mediumship and developed the German Uranian system of astrology that included 108 stars. Also, some of the ancient sages of China had also intuited some of the same knowledge eight thousand years ago, to develop the Four Pillars of Wisdom astrology containing 108 stars.

The Horary system of modern astrology in the West is, in the main, a false doctrine and an unreliable system of divination containing only the immediate solar orb and nine planets.

Star Pattern Practice:

1. Pick three star patterns each day within the correct quadrant (spring, summer, autumn, winter). As you gaze at the pattern, relax, inhale with the count of eight, and then exhale to the count of nine. This memory practice will begin to prepare the consciousness to actually receive the star-pattern energy at night at the appropriate season.

2. Memorize each star pattern name, with its essence quality and Vril sound as you gaze at the star shape. Memorize the Puuka location in the body. This practice can be done day or night.

Rengshalaat 2. The Star Practice

In the Magogik work, the second level of the Rengshalaat, the twelve ancient star patterns (before 100,000 years BC), contain the wisdom and spiritual consciousness beyond human experience. These patterns have been taken from the crystal of the capstone (the Gate of Tahar), originally mounted on top of the great pyramid of Giza in Egypt. These patterns correspond to constellations—alignments or corridors of cosmic space beyond the earth. The pyramid was not a tomb. It was a temple controlled by the priesthood and intended to provide passage to nether worlds for instructing and guiding the sacred line of pharaohs to rule Egypt wisely.

These patterns correspond to a type or shape and define a spiritual path for the right way to relate to reality. These patterns affect the neural pathways (nadis) and the right way of thinking. Doing these exercises will prepare the consciousness to receive and digest them. This allows the consciousness to make use of the special windows of spiritual opportunity. The practice of the great star wheel, which turns according to the precession of the equinoxes, defines a congress of heaven and earth, where both can come together in harmony. This practice also develops a sensitivity to the importance of the seasons.

These twelve patterns of star constellations are combined points of consciousness of unfallen stellar minds (parts of the original crystal of the original One Most High, a promise for those to return to the Divine Quantum. These unfallen stellar minds are dedicated to the recovery and return of the fallen Nom-Lu-Lu (original human souls) that were bound and trapped after the destruction of Tiamat in the fifth orbit of the Solar system. They reside within the earth (the sole remnant of that planet). As an aspirant, one must prepare to receive these energies that come only at specific windows of opportunity. These windows only appear at four times in a given year (the seasons), to integrate those energies into the subtle bodies. Also, as each Triad of patterns is integrated into the subtle bodies, at the solstice and equinox, all four triads are integrated into all of the subtle bodies.

1. Face the night sky and look for these patterns respective to the correct quadrant or season in the great wheel. Call up the name with its essence, and place with the shape into the appropriate Puuka. Utter the Vril silently, extending that into the appropriate subtle body.

2. Do the Rengshalaat 1 practice followed by the ruler practice before absorbing the star pattern triad energy of the appropriate quadrant.

Star Pattern Practice for Solstices and Equinoxes

1. Face the appropriate direction for each star pattern.

2. Call up the name with its essence and place that, with the shape, into the appropriate Puuka.

3. Utter the Vril silently from the unnamed organ, as the star pattern is visualized; extend that pattern to the

appropriate subtle body.

4. Do this practice at night. On the nights you do the Rengshalaat, do the star pattern practice after the animal and ruler exercises. On the Solstice and Equinox ceremony night, do this after the ceremony.

It is best to practice the triad group that leads up to the next Solstice and/or Equinox ceremony. Once a solstice or equinox is over, move on to the next triad to practice. For example, after doing the winter solstice ceremony, the next time the practice is done would be the first triad group, the vernal patterns.

Each triad window opens at a specific time (see the great wheel illustration)

The cycle will vary year to year, depending on the lunar cycle. Determine when both the full moon and the new moon is for each solstice and equinox ceremony.

The winter solstice window opens the day before the new moon. Practice each night beginning the night before the new moon until the night before the full moon, however many days that might be.

All other triad windows open from the day of the new moon until the day before the full moon. Do the practice each night, beginning the night of the new moon until the night before the full moon or solstice and/or equinox, whichever comes first.

There are two times a year when all twelve-star patterns are done on the same night. They are October 31 (Samhain) and April 30 (Beltane).

The Vernal Equinox is for the building of something or starting of something new. The intent is to plant the seeds for growth of something that is desired. It can be a new belief, or way of being, or spiritual growth in general. This season marks a period of accelerated growth. The ceremony should be done at sunrise.

The Summer Solstice is for creating a total alignment to the worlds of light at a time for deeper commitment to spiritual growth. This is about acknowledging the light and growth.

The Autumnal Equinox is for breaking of ties or old patterns. It is the period of harvest, the acknowledgement of things achieved and a period of great change, determining what no longer serves, seeking help to let go.

The Winter Solstice is for going inside to assess where is the state of being or the true internal condition. It is a period for deep internal reflection on the spiritual and emotional growth work needed. It is the period of the greatest darkness, of the highest intensity of the unseen cold force.

The Great Wheel, Magogik Power

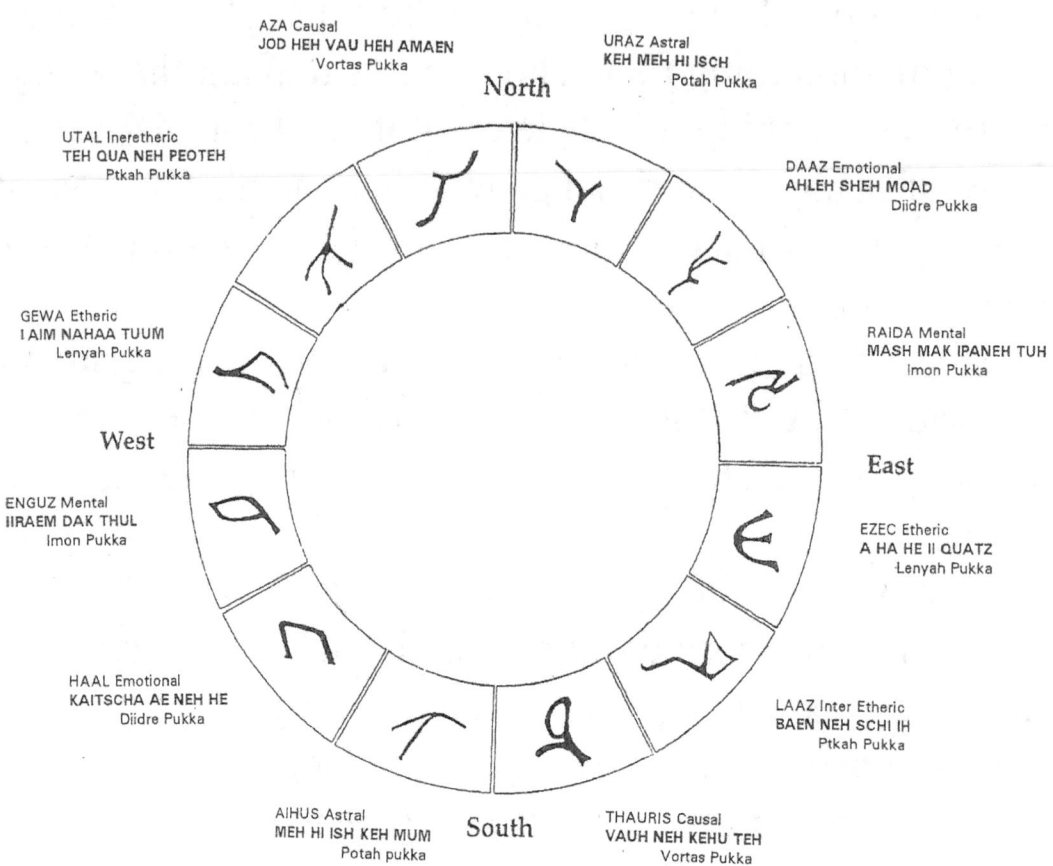

Star Wheel, Puukas and Constellations Illustration # 7

The Great Wheel, Magogik Power

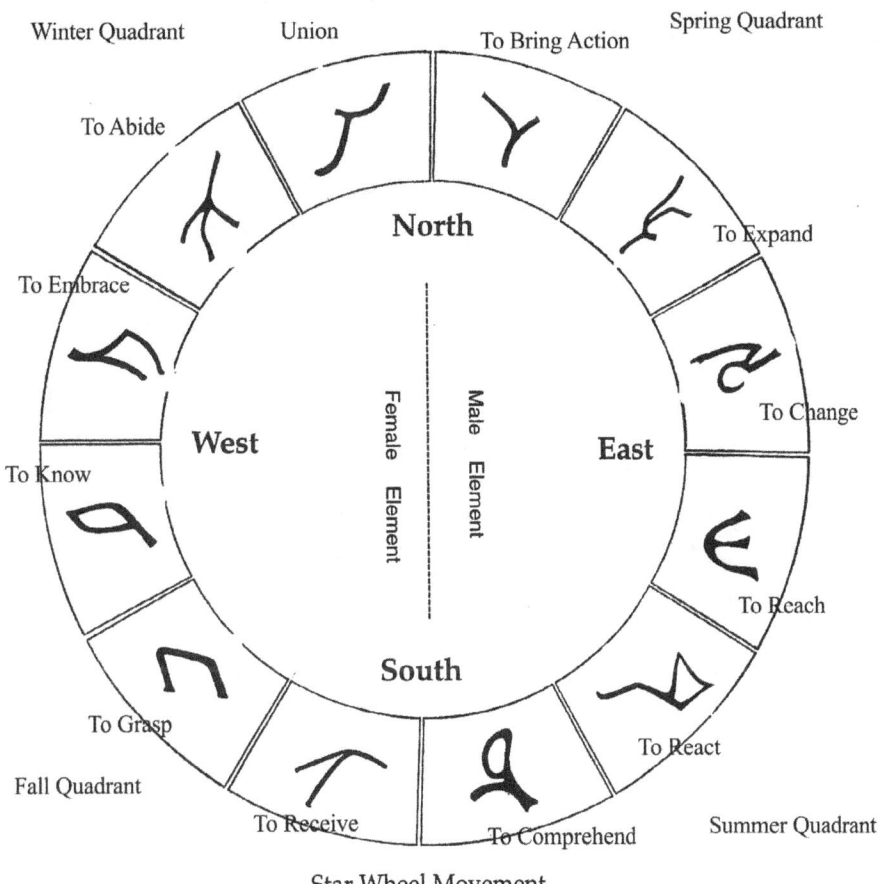

The Star Wheel with Constellations and Values Illustration # 8

The Great Wheel, Magogik Power

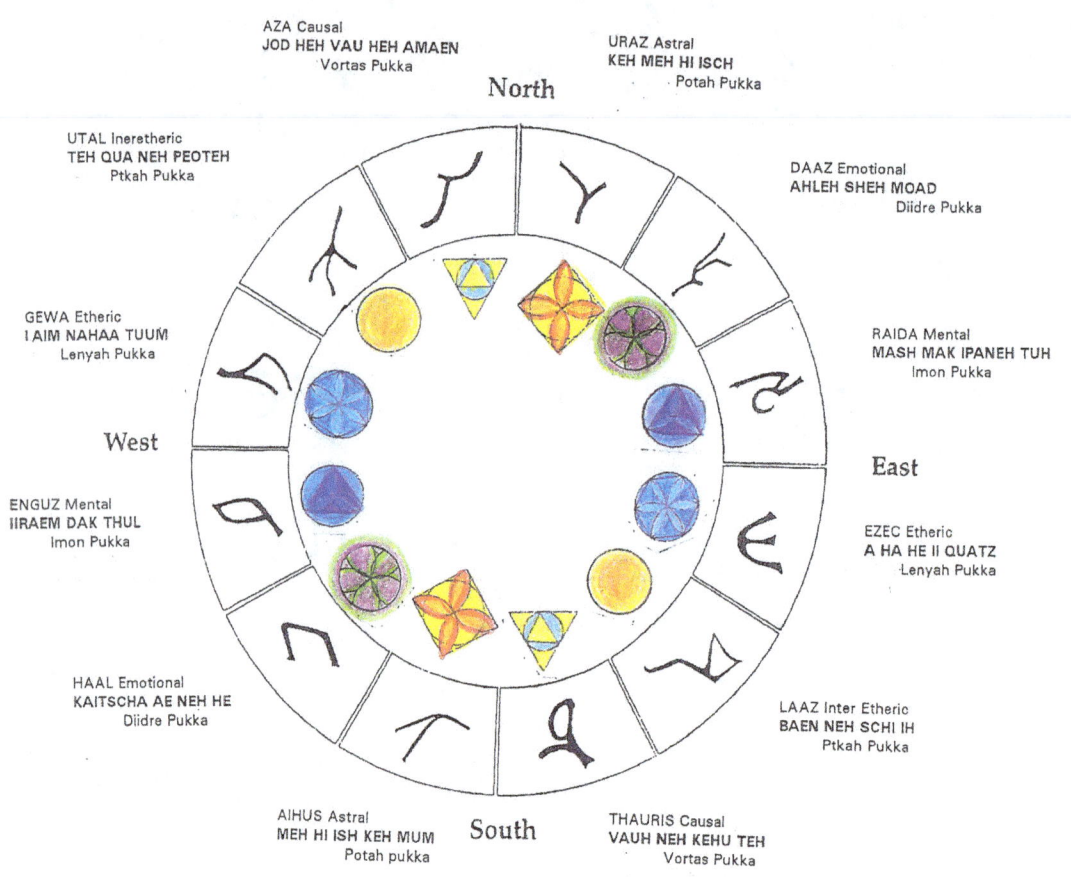

Star Wheel with Subtle bodies in each Quadrant Illustration # 9

The Great Wheel, Magogik Power

SPRING TRIAD - LOWER TRIANGLE

KEH MEh HIISH
URAZ
To bring action

Star Pattern # 2

Ahleh Sheh Moad
DAAZ
To Expand

Star Pattern # 3

Mashi Maak IPaneh Tuh
RAIDA
To Change

First Triad Spring Quadrant Illustration # 10

The Great Wheel, Magogik Power

 SUMMER TRIAD - UPPER TRIANGLE

AHa Heh IIQuatz
Ezec
To Reach

Star Pattern # 5

Baen Neh shII
LAAZ
To React

Star Pattern # 6

Vau Neh Kehuteh

Second Triad Summer Quadrant Illustration # 11

The Great Wheel, Magogik Power

SUMMER TRIAD - UPPER TRIANGLE

AHa Heh IIQuatz
Ezec
To Reach

Star Pattern # 5

Baen Neh shII
LAAZ
To React

Star Pattern # 6

Vau Neh Kehuteh
THAURIS
To comprehend

Third Triad Autumnal Quadrant Illustration # 12

 AUTUMNAL TRIAD- LOWER TRIANGLE

MEh HIISH KEH MUM
Aihus
To Receive Action

Star Pattern # 8

Kaucha aen neh heh
HAAL
To Grasp

Star Pattern # 9

IIRaew Dak Thul
ENGUZ
To Know

Fourth Triad Winter Quadrant Illustration # 13

The Great Wheel, Magogik Power

1 ST. TRIAD WINDOW = VERNAL (SPRING) = Male Side

1. Look at pattern, close eyes and store the shape.
2. Think about and FEEL the essence and place both the pattern and it's essence in the appropriate Pukka in your body.
3. Utter the Vril from unnamed organ SILENTLY as you visualize the star pattern and extend it to the appropriate subtle body.

3.
Name	Essence	Pukka	Subtle Body
RAIDA	TO CHANGE	IMON	MENTAL

VRIL = Mashi Maak IPaneh Tuh
(sounds like) MOSH MOCK EEPANEE TOO

2.
Name	Essence	Pukka	Subtle Body
DAAZ	TO EXPAND	DIIDRE (2" BELOW NAVEL)	EMOTIONAL

VRIL = AhLeh Sheh Moad
(sounds like) AH LEH SHEH MO AAD

1.
Name	Essence	Pukka	Subtle Body
URAZ	TO BRING ACTION	POTAH (PERINEUM)	ASTRAL

VRIL = KEH MEh HIISH
(sounds like) KEH MEH HE EESH

First Triad Spring Quadrant Practice Illustration # 14

The Great Wheel, Magogik Power

2ND. TRIAD WINDOW = SUMMER = Male Side

1. Look at pattern, close eyes and store the shape.

2. Think about and FEEL the essence and place both the pattern and it's essence in the appropriate Pukka in your body.

3. Utter the Vril from unnamed organ SILENTLY as you visualize the star pattern and extend it to the appropriate subtle body.

3.
Name	Essence	Pukka	Subtle Body
THAURIS	TO COMPREHEND	VORTAS (3rd. EYE)	CAUSAL

VRIL= Vau Neh Kehuteh
(sounds like) Voh Neh Keh oo Tay

2.
Name	Essence	Pukka	Subtle Body
LAAZ	TO REACT	PTKAH (THROAT)	INTER-ETHERIC

VRIL= Baen Neh shII
(sounds like) BayEEn Neh SHE EE

1.
Name	Essence	Pukka	Subtle Body
EZEC	TO REACH	LENYAH (HEART)	ETHERIC

VRIL= AHa Heh IIQuatz
(sounds like) AH HA Aeh EE QUATZ

Second Triad Summer Quadrant Practice Illustration # 15

The Great Wheel, Magogik Power

3RD. TRIAD WINDOW = AUTUMNAL = Female Side

1. Look at pattern, close eyes and store the shape.

2. Think about and FEEL the essence and place both the pattern and it's essence in the appropriate Pukka in your body.

3. Utter the Vril from unnamed organ SILENTLY as you visualize the star pattern and extend it to the appropriate subtle body.

3. | Name | Essence | Pukka | Subtle Body |
|---|---|---|---|
| ENGUZ | TO KNOW | IMON (SOLAR PLEXUS) | MENTAL |

Vril = llRaem Dak Thul
(sounds like) E E RAYEEM DOCK TOOL

2. | Name | Essence | Pukka | Subtle Body |
|---|---|---|---|
| HAAL | TO GRASP | DIIDRE (2" BELOW NAVEL) | EMOTIONAL |

Vril = Kaiicha Aen Neh Heh
(sounds like) KAYEECHA AEEN NEH HEH

1. | Name | Essence | Pukka | Subtle Body |
|---|---|---|---|
| AIHUS | TO RECEIVE ACTION | POTAH (PERINEUM) | ASTRAL |

Vril = MEh HIISH KEH MUM
(sounds like) MEH HE EESH KEH MOOM

Third Triad Autumnal Quadrant Practice Illustration # 16

4TH. TRIAD WINDOW = WINTER = Female Side

1. Look at pattern, close eyes and store the shape.

2. Think about and FEEL the essence and place both the pattern and it's essence in the appropriate Pukka in your body.

3. Utter the Vril from un-named organ SILENTLY as you visualize the star pattern and extend it to the appropriate subtle body.

3.
Name	Essence	Pukka	Subtle Body
AZA	UNION	VORTAS (BROW)	CAUSAL

VRIL = JodHeh VauHeh Amaen
(sounds like) JOD HEH VAU HEH AH MAIN

2.
Name	Essence	Pukka	Subtle Body
UTAL	TO ABIDE (Agree)	PTKAH (THROAT)	INTER-ETHERIC

VRIL = TehQua Neh Pehohte
(sounds like) TECK QUA NEH PAY OH TAY

1.
Name	Essence	Pukka	Subtle Body
GEWA	TO EMBRACE	LENYA (HEART)	ETHERIC

VRIL = Laim Nahaa Tuum
(sounds like) LAYEEM NAHAA TO OOM

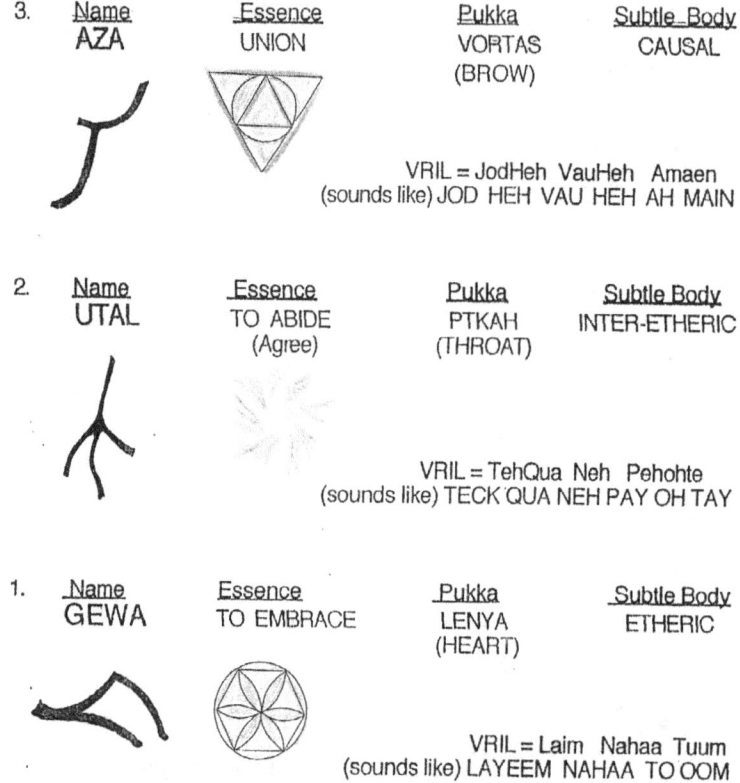

Fourth Triad Winter Quadrant Practice Illustration # 17

The Complete 12 Patter Star Wheel practice is done on this date:
Samhaine (Sam'ne-Nos Cyn Calan Gauaf) Eve of November 1st
Beltane (Bel'ne – Nos Cyn Cadi Haf) Eve of May 1st
All other dates which surround the precession of the Equinoxes is done with only those patterns relating to that season involving the windows of the Lunar Cycle.
See the Druid Year of Plieades Illustration.

Pole Star Meditation
Day practice: With the prism, take in the royal blue light into the left eye
(Left eye of Horus)
2-3 seconds. 9X
Each time, loosen the eyes and consciously seize the light, hold the color in the mind/heart and store it into the Lenya (heart)Puuka. Inside the blue light is the special geometric pattern from Askargon (the spirit of the Sun)
Night practice: (of the same day)
View the pole star (Polaris):
Fill each chamber of the pituitary (#1, #2 then #3-the belt of Orion) with the royal blue color stored from the day practice.
3X

Then Activate The Etheric subtle body (Lenya Puuka): Speak the Vril from the Etheric subtle body as the blue color is loaded into the chambers of the pituitary 3X.

Vril: Qu-ah Meh Nih Hah
　　　Seh-Poh-Shi-reh-reh-ah
　　　Neh -Pah-Vau-Pah
　　　Va-Leh-Eh-Oh-Besh-ud

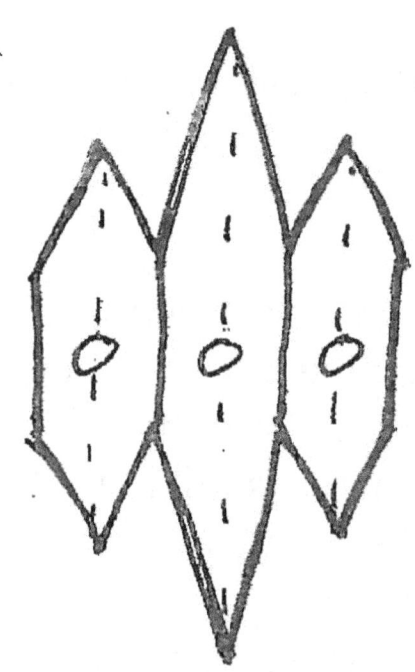

The Three Chambers of the Pituitary Illustration # 18

The Great Wheel, Magogik Power

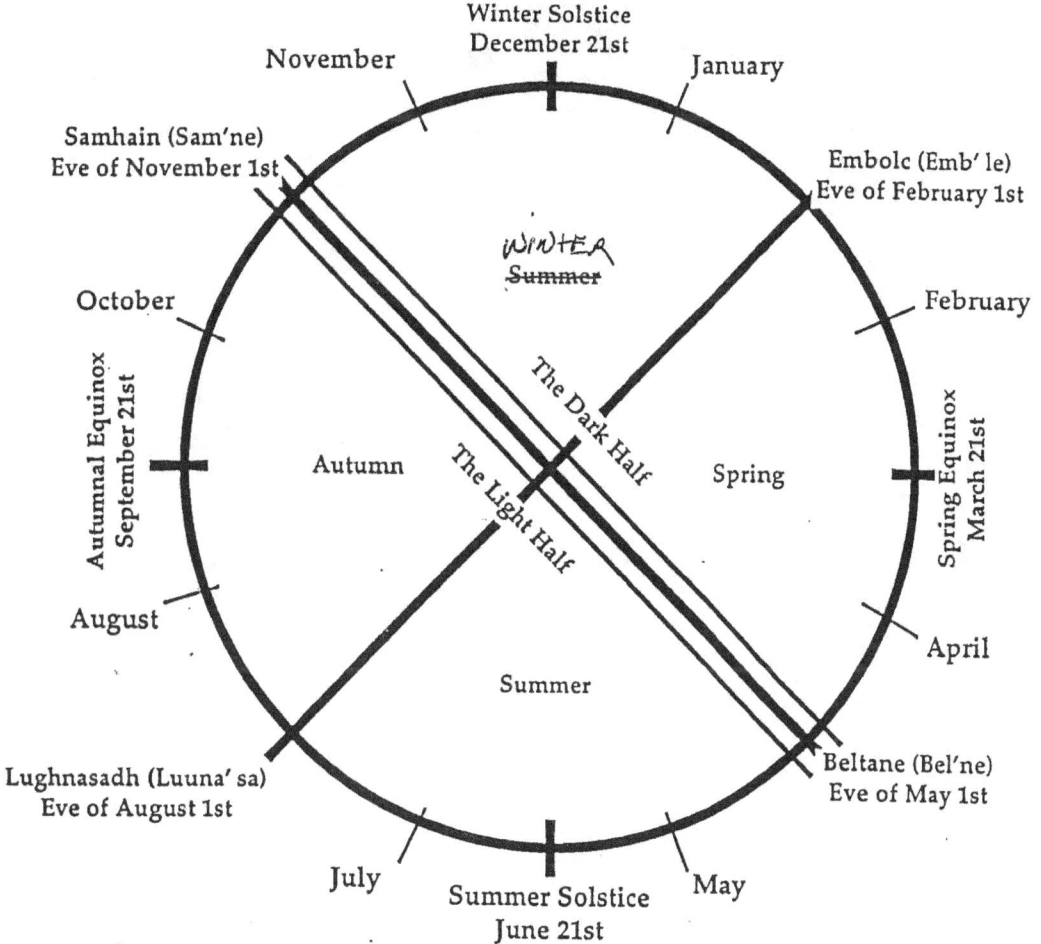

Druid Year of plieades Illustration # 19

The Great Wheel, Magogik Power

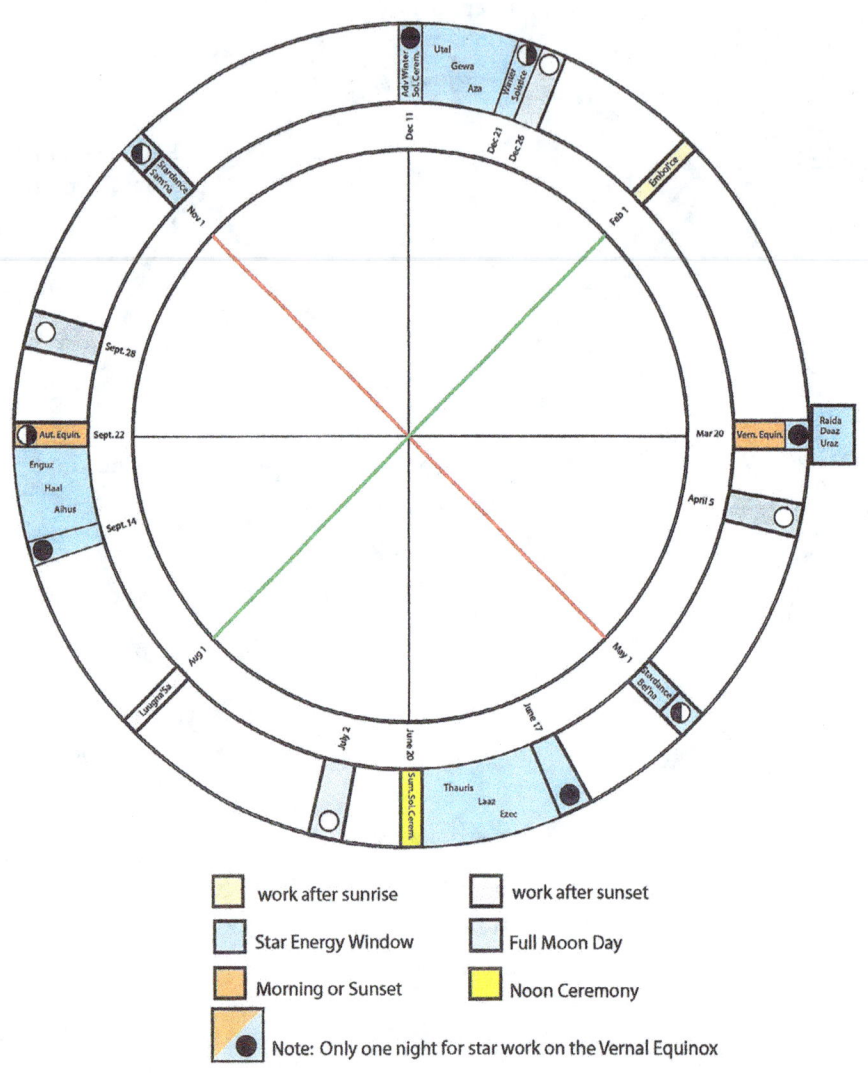

Druid Year Practice Chart Illustration # 20

The Puukas

In the Atlantean language, Puuka means window. Unlike other spiritual systems in Tibet, Eurasia, and Indo-Aryian locations, they describe these attributes differently and with a bit of distortion. They define these as point sources of energy, such as with the Indian term chakra. This is actually not accurate.

If you were to describe a window to someone with the sunlight coming through, you would not describe the window as a point source of energy. The window is a gateway for the light to pass through, whereas the real source is beyond the window. The window analogy falls short here because the window is not dynamic in its form but static. It cannot alter the view of light in any particular way other than reducing the amount of light that passes.

This is the basis of Atlantean spiritual work. They knew that the source of life, the living force and energy does not originate within the body but originates beyond the body. They believed that the body was not real in the sense of something physical.

Moreover, the so-called body is a complex energy field of multiple vibrations coalesced together into a form that reflects the essence of all reality.

Like the concept of a window, the window or Puuka has a specific form or shape, as they referred to it. That shape defines a particular vibrational view or dimension of that part of reality. The only similarity between the other systems is their relative position within the body shape.

There are plexuses or centers of neural networks in the physical point of view that become the sensors of each window, beginning at the base of the spine, rising to the plexus located just below the navel, then on up to the solar plexus, then the heart plexus, then the throat plexus, and then the plexus at the brow and finally at the crown at the top of the head. Not much information is given to the role of the spinal cord. These plexuses extend from the cord and increase in complexity of nerve fibers at each Puuka.

The spinal cord is not static either. It actually shrinks and extends in length responding to the vibrations of energy flowing into the cerebrospinal fluid. That fluid is actually highly refined blood. It functions like a continuously variable antenna, receiving and concentrating all those energies and delivering those energies to each plexus. The Puukas never close or stop. If they were to do so, then the form would cease to exist being cut off from reality.

In the Atlantean system, they are by themselves, not as important as how they interact with each other. In this spiritual system, the idea of balance is more important. The relative health of each Puuka is important as they interact with each other.

    The practices develop the balance that not only ensures a solid and healthy connection to the quantum universe and all of its dimensions but defines the level of awareness of those connections continuously. There are resonant sounds that relate to each Puuka's performance and vitality, which are discussed in the other chapters of this manual. Please look at the illustration for a visual display of their locations. These Puukas were named from the perineum to the crown respectively.

    The Potah Puuka at the perineum, the Diidre Puuka at the navel, the Imon Puuka at the solar plexus, the Lenyah Puuka at the heart, the Ptkah Puuka at the throat, the Vortas Puuka at the brow or third eye. The crown Puuka remained unnamed in respect to the Most High that has no name, or the Quantum (The Way).

ASTRAL BODY

```
 F   F   F  B  B  B
LEH AH MEH EE REH EH
```

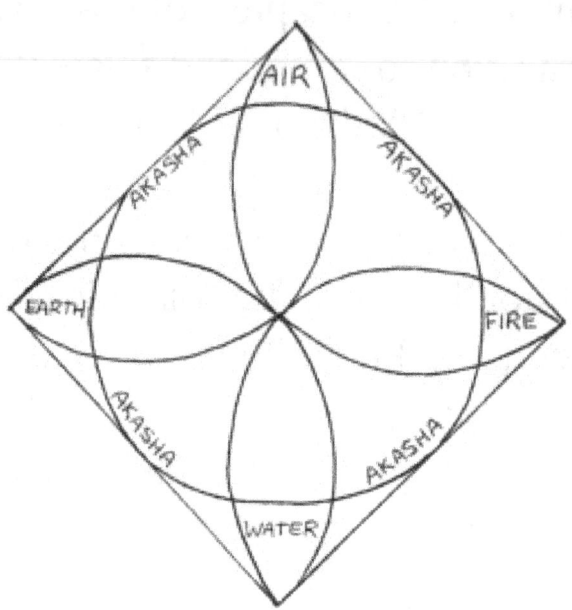

YELLOW WITH ORANGE HALO

KEY: F F F B B B

AS IT RELATES TO THE ENERGY FLOW PATTERN FOR THE SUBTLE BODY ALIGNMENT PRACTICE

Druid Year of plieades Illustration # 21

MENTAL BODY

SEH OH LEH VAU AH OOH TEH

KEY: G G G G A A A
AS IT RELATES TO THE ENERGY FLOW PATTERN FOR THE
SUBTLE BODY ALIGNMENT PRACTICE

Druid Year of plieades Illustration # 22

EMOTIONAL BODY

```
 C   C   C   E   E   E
VAU AH BEH EH MEH EE
```

KEY: C C C E E E
AS IT RELATES TO THE ENERGY FLOW PATTERN FOR
THE SUBTLE ALIGNMENT PRACTICE

Druid Year of plieades Illustration # 23

ETHERIC BODY

A A A A G G G
SEH OH LEH REH EH TEH OH

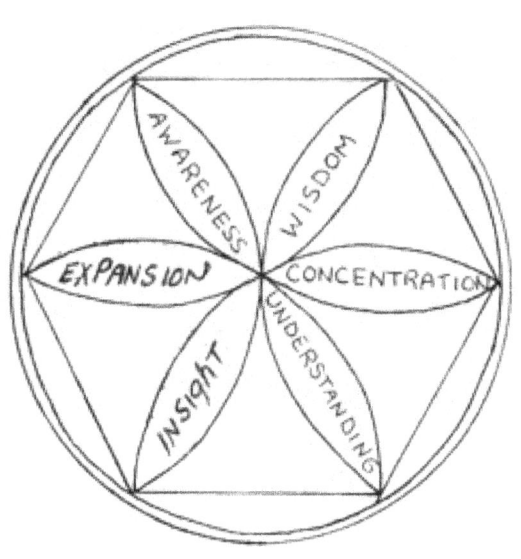

KEY: A A A A G G G
AS IT RELATES TO THE ENERGY FLOW PATTERN FOR THE
SUBTLE BODY ALIGNMENT PRACTICE

Druid Year of plieades Illustration # 24

CAUSAL BODY OCTAVE #1

```
 B   B   B   F   F   F
VAU AH OOH TEH TEH OH
```

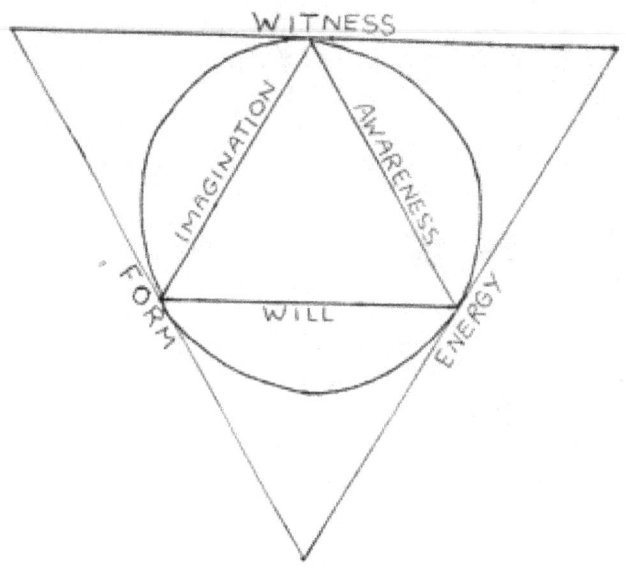

KEY: B B B F F F
AS IT RELATES TO THE ENERGY FLOW PATTERN FOR THE
SUBTLE BODY ALIGNMENT PRACTICE

Druid Year of plieades Illustration # 25

Hand Mudras

In the human body, there are two primary nervous networks; first is the sympathetic system, which governs thinking, seeing, hearing, walking, talking, and eating. Then there is the parasympathetic system, which governs all of the autonomic functions, such as lungs, heart, kidneys, spleen, pancreas, the endocrine glands, and certain digestive functions in the alimentary canal. Both of these nervous networks are tied into the main channel or nervous system highway called the spinal cord.

Mudras are hand gestures utilized to facilitate specific neuronal/nadis responses within the body having to do with meridians, not necessarily relating directly to the nervous systems.

Besides the nerve networks throughout the body, there are also implied impulses that relate to nervelike pathways or channels. These are not nerve ganglia per se, but energy channels that govern another form of energy, called the life force, (also known in Asian philosophy as chi), which classical medical science is still in the process of accepting. These are the channels with nodal points throughout the body, identified by Asian medical science as acupuncture points, and their pathways are called meridians.

All living systems have these meridians. Even the Earth is now considered an eco- or life system that is very much alive and dependent on these same kind of meridians, except they are called ley lines on the earth. The lower heaven (not the upper heaven or star realm outside of the Earth's atmosphere) also has corresponding pathways called Agogik or cold magnetic lines, better known as the magnetic lines of the Earth's field.

In the Atlantean spiritual understanding, these were referred to as the pathways of the earth dragon and the sky dragon.

In the human form, there is a corresponding set of pathways that exists within the body. The meridian channels have both male (Agogik) and female (Magogik) paths that intertwine throughout the body, and the places where they meet are the nodes referred to as points. In the normal, healthy human, these channels are open to both the earth and sky energy and find their balance at the nodal points, and these are the Perruiti Rogalin or neutral points.

At this time, our Western medical sciences have not created instrumentalities that can detect these energies in the body. So, ipso facto, if they cannot be detected, they are nonexistent and perceived as false science.

Unfortunately, Western medical sciences are still perceiving the human body as a machine controlled by the anima, or the will of human consciousness. This is a mechanical view, much like Niels Bohr, who first envisioned the atomic structure as a set of marbles or particles (the particle theory) as the basis for matter developed before the advent of quantum theory (the wave theory). A kind of compromise was realized by stating the particles can act as waves in one moment and particles in another moment. German physicist Max Planck won the Nobel Prize in 1918 for his discoveries, then followed by Einstein, Schrodinger, Dirac, and others, further developing the quantum mechanics that we have today.

Better known in the Indo-Aryan and Euro-Asian cultures, the idea of hand gestures or mudras is well accepted within many spiritual systems of practice, such as in the practice of yoga, whether it be Tibetan or Indian. Curiously, these mudras are not explained and further defined for their specific purposes.

The ancient spiritual practice of Magik (not sleight-of-hand magic used by stage performers in the West) is the real ancient practice of sorcery, well known in Egypt and practiced by the priesthood of Karnak.

This fact is even recorded in the canon text of the Bible as described in Exodus, when Moses performed miracles, such as when the priesthood converted their staffs into vipers, Moses converted his staff to a viper also, and his serpent consumed their serpents, thus proclaiming his power (supposedly originating from the "one true God") to be greater than theirs.

The fact not well known is, before Moses was exiled from Egypt by Ramses, he was also raised in the pharaoh's palace by Pharaoh Ceti the First, groomed to be his replacement after his death; as pharaoh-elect, he had been trained in the priesthood before his exile. So, he possessed the same knowledge of this power.

In the same fashion, in Gaul (known today as France) the Druids, in particular, the Merlyns (a Druidic name for shaman) practiced hand gestures also utilized to create mists and other forms of weather control for the knights of the realm, such as Uther Pendragon. Later, these Merlyns tried to help defeat the Roman invaders of Gaul as well.

Mudras are used to control the flow of life force in specific pathways that give rise to fields of energy extending well past the boundaries of the human body. These gestures arise from specific fingertips that touch together to redirect the life force. The classic yogic mudra of the thumb and index finger joined during meditation is designed to calm the mind and body for meditation and concentration.

The more dynamic form is used in martial arts to act as a force against an opponent in battle such as aikido, gung fu

Hand Mudras

hing si, and chi kung. During the Boxer Rebellion in China, martial artists used chi kung called the Iron Shirt or Balloon Man, creating a shield around the body, providing a defense against bullets. It was reported that it took dozens of bullets shot at each of the rebels before they fell dead.

In the Euro-Asian practice of sorcery, mudra forces were manifested to cause calamities, hexes, and deadly attacks against foes. Whereas the positive use of mudras can promote healing of wounds, raising the dead (in the case of Lazarus raised up by Jeshua), also trained in Asia and Tibet during his long absence before beginning his ministry. These gospel details were removed from the canons and considered by Alexander the Great as heretical texts during the ecumenical council of Mycenea in the fourth century AD.

Mudras are an essential part of the Atlantean spiritual practice of Rengmeatralaat (sitting meditation) and the minor circle movement, combining the heavenly force and earthly force into the body for later use. They are described here with illustrations.

Hand Mudras

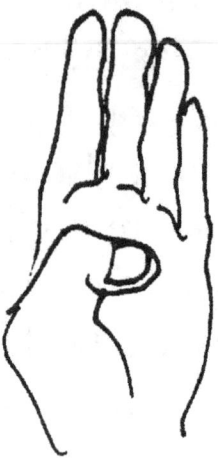

MAADU Mudra
Sleeping Moon

Diagram #1

Tazua Mudra
Poking the Shadow

Diagram #2

Tazua Mudra Illustration # 27

Hand Mudras

Plake Mudra
Spitting Water

Diagram #3

Plake Mudra Illustration # 28

Hand Mudras

95

Mazat Mudra
Grasping the Moon

Diagram #4

Mazat Mudra Illustration # 29

96   Hand Mudras

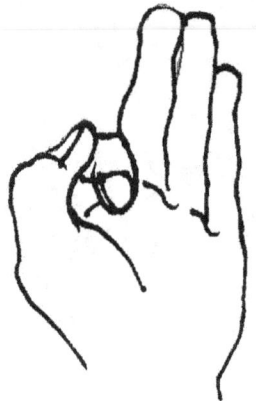

Medak Mudra
Silencing the Sparrow

Diagram #5

Medak Mudra Illustration # 30

Hand Mudras

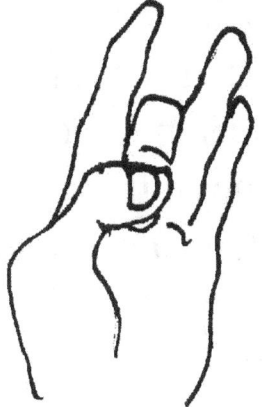

Buutok Mudra
Harvesting the Seeds

Diagram #6

Buutok Mudra Illustration # 31

Quaternary Placement, First Octave

This practice stresses the importance of establishing the vibrational placement, what my master calls Quaternary placement. The individual needs to identify where one is in three-dimensional vibrational space. This is done by voweling in four directions over a power point, meaning where at least two ley lines cross, as well as tuning oneself with the heavenly and earthly energies and the obvious polarity. In this way, one can plot their way vibrationally, and then one can align the subtle bodies and then go to any given plane of consciousness. It is called creating a point of origin. This enables one to establish where one is on the being level and then alter the vibration of the being and go to another place and/or time.

In order to reach the subtle bodies, one has to start somewhere. The individual will be taking the next step toward cooperating with the elemental forces to accomplish some changes in their life by identifying vibrationally where they are. In so doing, the individual will be able to create a power point or spot on the Earth. This is important for all aspirants. This action can be used at all solstice and equinox practices. With practice, the individual will be able to recall from memory each of the four directions for tone, Vril element, and color, as well as the vowel sounds for heaven and for earth.

1. Start by facing east, and remember the tone for two minutes, then say out loud the vowel sound Ah, which is the sound for the element of air. Then sing the Vril pattern silently from the unnamed organ in the throat with the lips slightly parted while imagining the feeling and color of the element associated with that direction.

2. The eyes will move only for this practice to the next direction in a clockwise order. Follow the directions as shown in the illustration for each direction but only the eyes will move toward each direction. Then follow the instructions for the vowel sounds of heaven and earth.

a. East – air, eyes straight forward

Vowel Ah (say out loud then silently)

Tone of C

Color – light blue

Vril-Ah-Che-Leh-Heh (speak silently)

Then follow the instructions for each subtle body.

b. South – Fire, eyes look to the right

Vowel EEE (say out loud then silently)

Tone D

Color – Deep red and orange

Vril-Shi-Heh-Seh-Teh (speak silently)

Then follow the instructions for each subtle body.

c. West – Water, eyes look back behind the head

Vowel Ooh (say out loud then silently)
Color – Violet with silver striations
Vril – Meh-Neh-Vau-Geh (speak silently)
Then follow the instructions for each subtle body.
d.   North – Earth, eyes look to the left
Vowel Iee (speak out loud then speak silently)
Tone E
Color – forest green with red and orange striations
Vril – Er-Ee-Vau-Reh (speak silently)
Then follow the instructions for each subtle body.

e.   Heaven – shift the eyes upward while taking a breath through the nose into to the abdomen
Vowel Eh and tone F; lift up the heels

f.   Earth – shift the eyes down while exhaling through the nose into the abdomen
Vowel Oh with the tone of B
See the illustrations.

QUATERNARY PLACEMENT PRACTICE

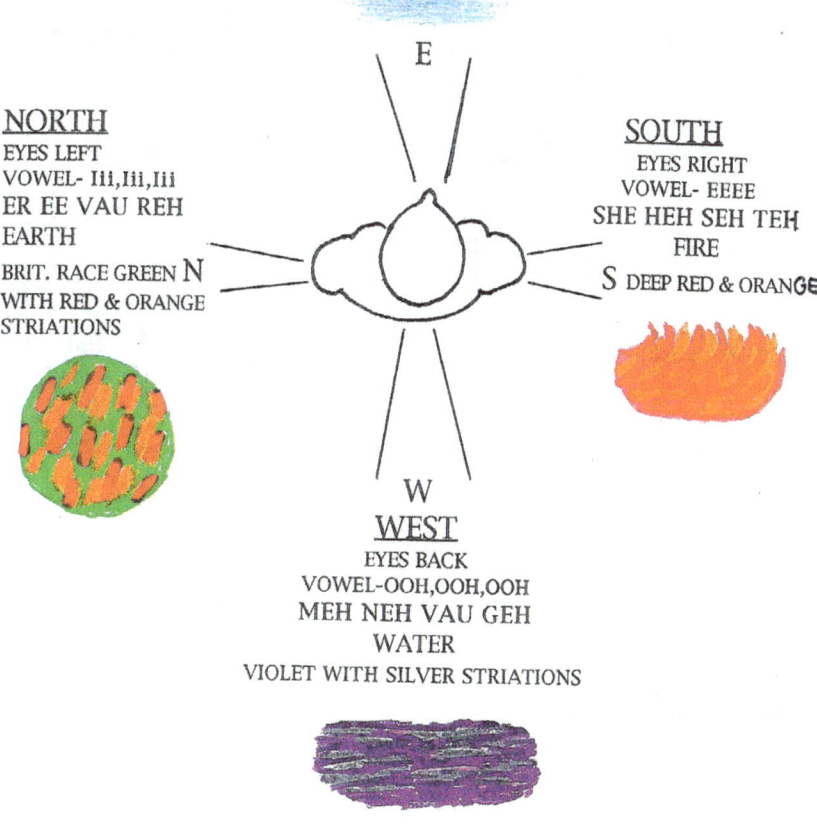

EAST
EYES STRAIGHT
VOWEL-AH, AH, AH
VRIL-AH CHE LEH HEH
AIR
COLOR- LIGHT BLUE

NORTH
EYES LEFT
VOWEL- Iii, Iii, Iii
ER EE VAU REH
EARTH
BRIT. RACE GREEN WITH RED & ORANGE STRIATIONS

SOUTH
EYES RIGHT
VOWEL- EEEE
SHE HEH SEH TEH
FIRE
DEEP RED & ORANGE

WEST
EYES BACK
VOWEL-OOH, OOH, OOH
MEH NEH VAU GEH
WATER
VIOLET WITH SILVER STRIATIONS

Quaternary Placement Illustration # 32

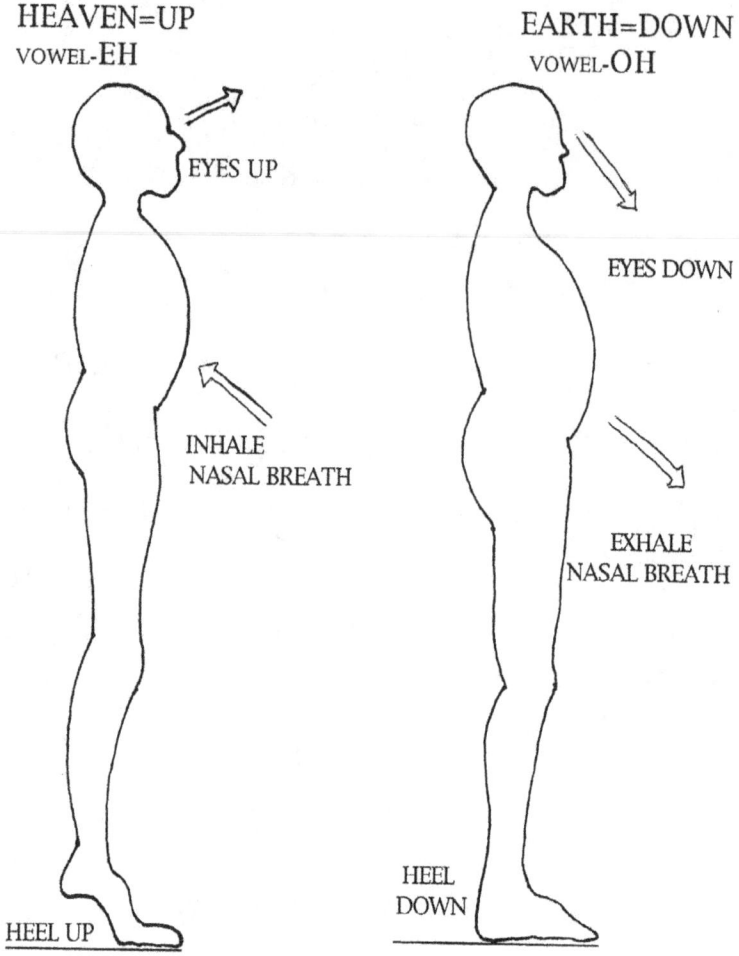

Quaternary Placement Vril Tones Illustration # 33

The Minor Circle, The Buuor Shai

The Minor Circle or Cycle of the Buuor Shai is an extension of the Quaternary Placement and Subtle Body Alignment. This part of the work represents the second octave of defining the placement of the soul during the various procedures, or in other words, where the individual soul begins the work.

This second octave represents who is beginning the work. The Buuor Shai addresses the polarized feelings as they enter into the Torax meditation. So, it becomes clearer that to unravel the knots of the heart, the feelings need to be neutral. The Buuor Shai establishes further clarity as to the true origin of feelings in the soul as an emotional movement of the emotional subtle body.

Through the proper application of this practice, the individual can separate the feeling from the creation/identification marker that is set by the soul upon its origination. In turn, this helps the soul observe the creation of the feeling from its origin and thus set some distance between the soul and the feeling. This will reveal who is feeling the emotional energy movement. This helps to further separate the soul from the identification of its true identity to the signature essence of the feeling.

The benefits of this part of the training are that time will begin to stop during the process. The process of aging as a human factor manifest in the body as trauma can be halted and even reversed in the individual. The consciousness of the soul imprint is elevated to reveal to itself how precisely the feelings bind the consciousness in each individual case.

Later, as the individual continues to practice the quaternary placement (the "where") and the Buuor Shai (the "who"), a third octave, Spiral of the Quihl Shai, arises within all of the subtle bodies naturally as (the "what") which is present. Then, all three octaves proceed toward the rest of the practices.

1.   Set up the quaternary placement with the four cardinal points

A.   Face the east:

a.   Call up a feeling and couple to the energy of the east, then circulate the consciousness clockwise (counterclockwise for the female)

B.   Face the south

a.   Couple the feeling to the south, and continue to rotate clockwise, dragging the energy of the east and joining those with the energy of the south.

C.   Face the west

a.   Couple the feeling with that of the east and the south, and rotate clockwise to the west, adding the western energy and feeling.

D.   Face the north

a.   Rotate clockwise to the north, dragging the other directional energies and the feeling.

2.   Rotate the feeling with the four directions faster and faster until there is a sense of joining together to merge as one flat plane. Continue until there is a sense of vertical separation between the individual and the feeling.

Rengshalaat First Octave, the Animal Forms

Rengshalaat principles of the Atlantean Temple represent the shadow side of an alchemical process that works closely on and within the physical body. Not unlike the use of the Quaternary Placement principles, this practice also utilizes the cold magnetic forces of the Earth in a different way, through the Agogik energy.

This practice involves the simulation of specific animal attributes through forms and movements reflecting certain animal behavior. Putting the physical body into this uncommon behavior stimulates certain parts of the body and mind that enhance or increase the development of evolutionary reactions. Specifically, these movements relate to the male aspect of bodily fluids, which directly involve and have an impact on psychic development.

Within the nerve pathways of the body, nervelike tissues called Nadis have certain pathways functioning in ways, in the normal sense, to regulate bodily functions corresponding to procreative purpose.

In this first octave, the individual begins the stimulus techniques that will offer subtle changes to organs and glands, which have a "night side" or "shadow side" of functioning that are normally dormant. These movements separate the normal functions and redirect those organs and glands toward their extraordinary function. These extraordinary functions are unknown to the West in the modern era. The Asian and Indo-Aryan cultures have some of this knowledge buried within esoteric texts long since forgotten or lost, existing beyond or outside of the known world.

These patterns of behavior and movement awaken unknown vibrations by interacting with the Earth's cold magnetic force, causing the body to respond in like kind, giving rise to strange and unusual responses and awakening hidden properties that help the evolutionary process to higher states of consciousness and being.

These practices prepare the individual for receiving cosmic vibrations originating from the constellation patterns that arise during each quadrant of the great wheel, the precession of the equinoxes. That process then is continued in the second octave called Rengshalaat 2, the practice of absorbing the star patterns into the subtle bodies, which are later digested in the final octave of Rengshalaat 3, called Rengmiatralaat. Rengshalaat 1 practice needs to be done two to three times per week, weather permitting, followed by the Regshalaat 2 star practice for the quadrant that is available. Note: Rengmiatralaat 3 sitting meditation cannot be practiced until at least one full passage of the great wheel is completed. The exercises should be done after dark and outside whenever possible, without artificial lighting. Candles can be used for the practice similar to the dragon's breath practice. The practitioner can do one to two animals at a time, just so all of the animal forms are done at least once in any seven-day period.

Cleaning the auric field:
Take a shower before practice. Before entering the water, clap the hands together at the throat level, then bring the hands up above the head and then quickly down the front of the body, sweeping the hands out and away from the body at the waist. While in the water, allow the water to strike the top of the head while running freely down the front and back of the body simultaneously.

Closing the auric field: (weaving the basket)
Before starting the practice, it is best to close the auric field. Use the imagination to visualize energy belts about eight to ten inches wide, and wrap the body, making a complete circle around the body like a mummy, starting at the solar plexus. The life force will follow the conscious thought and imagination. Wrap the body from head to toe, first clockwise then counterclockwise, weaving one over the other like a basket.

Cycling the breath:
a. Inhale, focusing on the crown nine counts.
b. Then focus on the brow and exhale five counts.
c. Then concentrate on the throat five counts.
d. Inhale, focusing on the brow nine counts.
e. Exhale, focusing on the crown five counts.
f. Then focus on the throat nine counts.

This set constitutes one cycle.

Begin this practice between three and nine cycles until twenty-seven cycles can be done.

Use of the Ruler:

The ruler has the purpose to focus and concentrate the magnetic energy as well as smooth out the energy after other practices are done, such as Rengshalaat first octave and the Dragon's Breath.

The ruler has three movements:

First movement:

     The ruler is held by both hands that are cupped over the ends. It starts by holding the ruler in the lap across the legs in a horizontal position near the hips and/or pelvis. Then, while inhaling a long, slow breath, the right end of the ruler is raised off of the legs and rotated on end across the chest to the left in a counterclockwise fashion, until it is perpendicular onto the left thigh with the left hand on the bottom supporting the ruler, as the right hand and arm swing over until the right arm is now horizontal across the chest and cupping the top of the ruler, while it is vertical and in front of and to the left of the left shoulder.

Then, on the exhale of the breath, long and slow, the ruler is lowered back to the lap into the horizontal starting position while rotating clockwise past the chest to the starting position near the hips and/or pelvis.

Then, inhaling a long and slow breath, the left end of the ruler is raised up off of the legs and rotated on end across the chest to the right in a clockwise fashion, until it is perpendicular onto the right thigh with the right hand on the bottom supporting the ruler, as the left hand and arm swing over until the left arm is horizontal across the chest and cupping the top of the ruler, while it is vertical and in front of and to the right of the right shoulder.

Then, on the exhale of the breath, long and slow, the ruler is lowered back to the lap into the horizontal starting position while rotating counterclockwise past the chest to the starting position near the hips and/or the pelvis.

This constitutes a complete round to the left and to the right. (This should be done three times.)

Second movement:

Stand while the ruler is held in front of the hips in a

horizontal position by both hands cupping the ends of the ruler. As the body is rotated at the waist slightly to the left, then an average step is taken forward by the left leg and foot, while at the same time, bending over and pushing the ruler down, keeping it horizontal and sweeping close to the left leg and thigh until the lower part of the shin, near the ankle, is reached. Then pull the ruler upward along the left leg, while keeping it horizontal, sweeping it close to the left leg until it returns to the waist and the body is again upright. (Note: Do not bring the ruler any higher, close to the heart.)

    Then rotate the body at the waist slightly to the right, then an average step is taken forward by the right leg and foot, while at the same time, bending over and pushing the ruler down, keeping it horizontal, sweeping close to the right leg and thigh until the lower part of the shin, near the ankle, is reached. Then pull the ruler upward along the right leg, while keeping it horizontal, sweeping it close, to the right leg until it returns to the waist and the body is again upright. (Note: Do not bring the ruler any higher, close to the heart.) This constitutes a complete round to the left and to the right. (This should be done two times after the first movement.)
Animal forms:
1.   Snake/Dragon (works on pituitary and thyroid together) Sit with feet flat on the floor. Breathe in to the count of nine,

widen the tongue, and press it to the back of the throat. Grimace and cross the eyes, protrude the jaw forward, and exhale through the nose forcefully to the count of eight while focusing on the brow. Then focus on the throat for eight counts. Do these three to nine times until twenty-seven repetitions can be done.

2. Cat (works on thyroid and pericardium meridians) While sitting in a chair, reach out with the right hand in a grabbing fashion as you inhale to the count of nine while rotating the hand, and the fingers and thumb are squeezed together. As you pull the hand back to the body, begin the exhale to the count of eight while extending the left hand out straight (fingers extended like a claw) and make a hissing sound with the focus on the throat, sticking out the tongue during the hissing sound.

Then, while the left hand is extended, begin to inhale to the count of nine, and rotate the hand while the fingers and thumb are squeezed together. Pull back the hand to the body, and begin to exhale to the count of eight while extending the right hand out straight (fingers extended like a claw) and make a hissing sound with the focus on the throat, sticking out the tongue during the hissing sound. Continue this cycle of pumping with each arm and hand three to nine cycles until twenty-seven cycles can be done.

3.   Bear: (works on the limbic and lymph system)
Stand with the toes turned inward and knees bent, arms loose with the hands facing palms away, wrists drawn tight so fingers are pulled up and arms slightly bent, shoulders forward, leaning forward from the waist with the lower jaw open and forward. Begin to inhale to the count of nine while weaving to the left; then, while growling, exhale to the count of eight while weaving back to center. Repeat this movement to the right and continue rolling back and forth as a bear would do in the challenging position.
(Note: It's good to watch a bear doing this.) Focus on the back of the head. This movement brings neutralizing force to the limbic and amygdala to reduce the impact of resistance and reptilian instinct.

4.   Monkey/Wolf: (works on kidneys, adrenals, and lung meridians)
Sit like an aboriginal Bushman, butt between the legs and arms in the middle, with the palms on the ground, fingers of each hand facing the other. Inhale to the count of nine; then, with the eyes looking up at the brow, pull lips forward to form a protruded oval shape, arch the back, and make a sound of ooh with the voice while exhaling to the count of eight. This is done three to nine times until twenty-seven can be done.

5. **Eagle:** (works with crown and adrenals)
Stand with the feet shoulder-width apart and knees slightly bent; backs of hands should be touching and held in front of the belly with elbows bent. Eyes are focused on the crown; begin to inhale to the count of eight while drawing the hands up the front of the body, and begin to rotate them inward. When the heart level is reached as the tips of fingers point to the heart, then continue upward until they reach the throat, at which time the hands separate while extending the arms out and away from the body like spreading the wings apart. Keeping the elbows bent, spread the fingers wide apart and begin to exhale through the nose to the count of nine while making a pecking motion at an imaginary egg above the head. Then gather all of the saliva in the mouth and swallow it with a gulp. Then drop the hands down and repeat. Do this three to nine times until twenty-seven repetitions can be done.

Rengmiatralaat, The Sitting Meditation

The techniques involved in the Rengmaitralaat Shadow Practice (sitting meditation) describes the inner path of Magogik energy recalled out of the subtle bodies from the outer path of Magogik stored in the star practice.

This means to resurrect the energy of the star patterns, which have been stored during the year at each quadrant during Rengshalaat practice, calling them up internally in the sitting movement. This is done daily. So, the individual soul regenerates the unfallen consciousness within the individual matrix of consciousness that exists in the soul in the present incarnation.

As the sitting meditation is performed, each pattern is called up into the consciousness along with its appropriate mudra, and each mudra is alternating from right to left and left to right while the individual is monitoring the breathing; of inhaling to the right as the hand gestures (mudras) move to the right and exhaling to the left as the hand gestures (mudras) move to the left.

The six mudras are also performed during the Bel'taine and Sam'haine ceremonies on each hand. So, the star patterns have their seed elements buried deep within the undeveloped consciousness of the individual soul, thus completing the full cycle of influence of the Magogik energy.

The practice is as follows.

1. The breathing technique:
a. inhale to the right
b. exhale to the left

    2. Use the mudras—implementing the abiding principle:

      i. Right-hand movement (left to right)

Uraz.	Daaz.	Raida
(astral).	(emtional).	(mental)
(potah)	(diidre)	(imon)
Ezec	Laaz	Thauris
(etheric)	(inter-Etheric)	(causal)
(lenya)	(ptkah)	(vortas)

      ii. Left-hand movement (right to left)

Aihus	Haal	Enguz
(astral)	(emotional)	(mental)
(potah)	(diidre)	(imon)
Gewa	Utal	Aza
(etheric)	(inter-etheric)	(causal)
(lenya)	(ptkah)	(vortas)

Rengmiatralaat, The Sitting Meditation

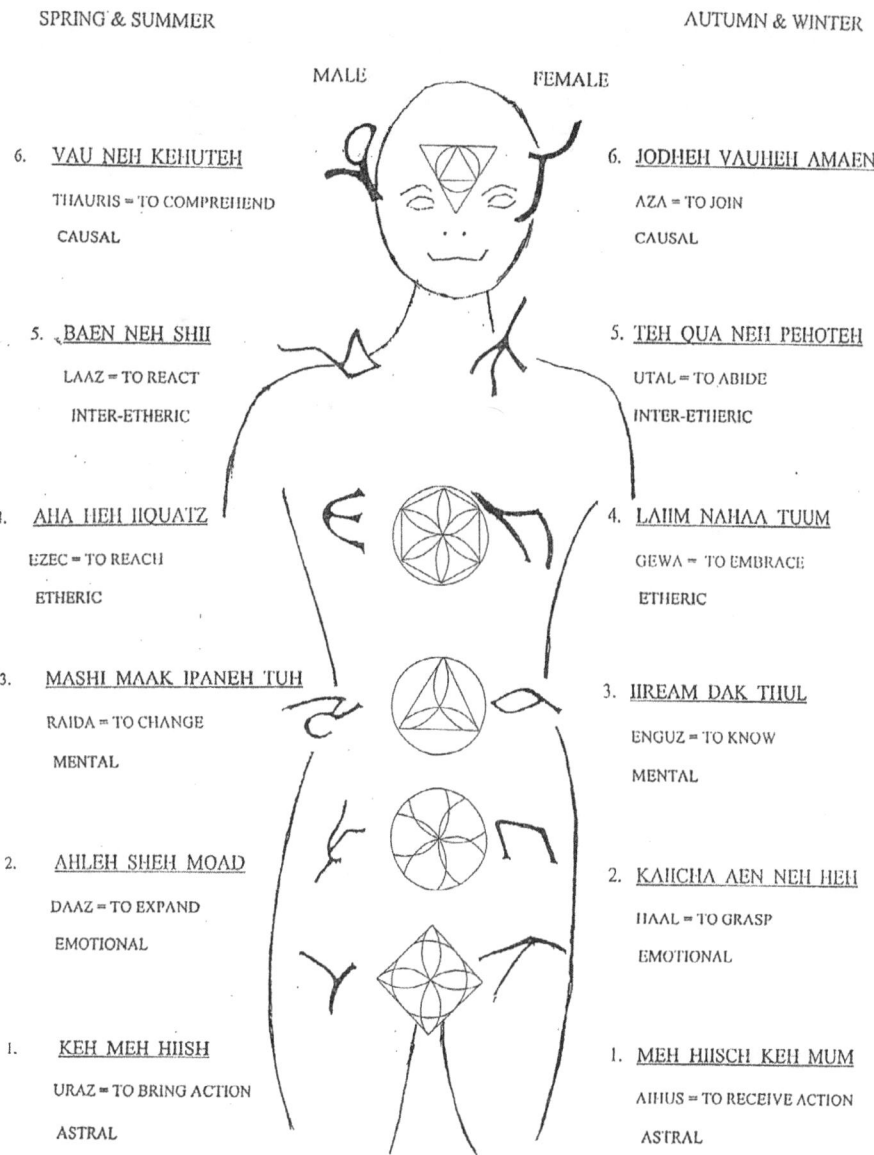

Rengmiatralaat Illustration # 33

Rengmiatralaat, The Sitting Meditation

Rengmiatralaat Illustration # 34

Rengshalaat First Octave, The Animal Forms

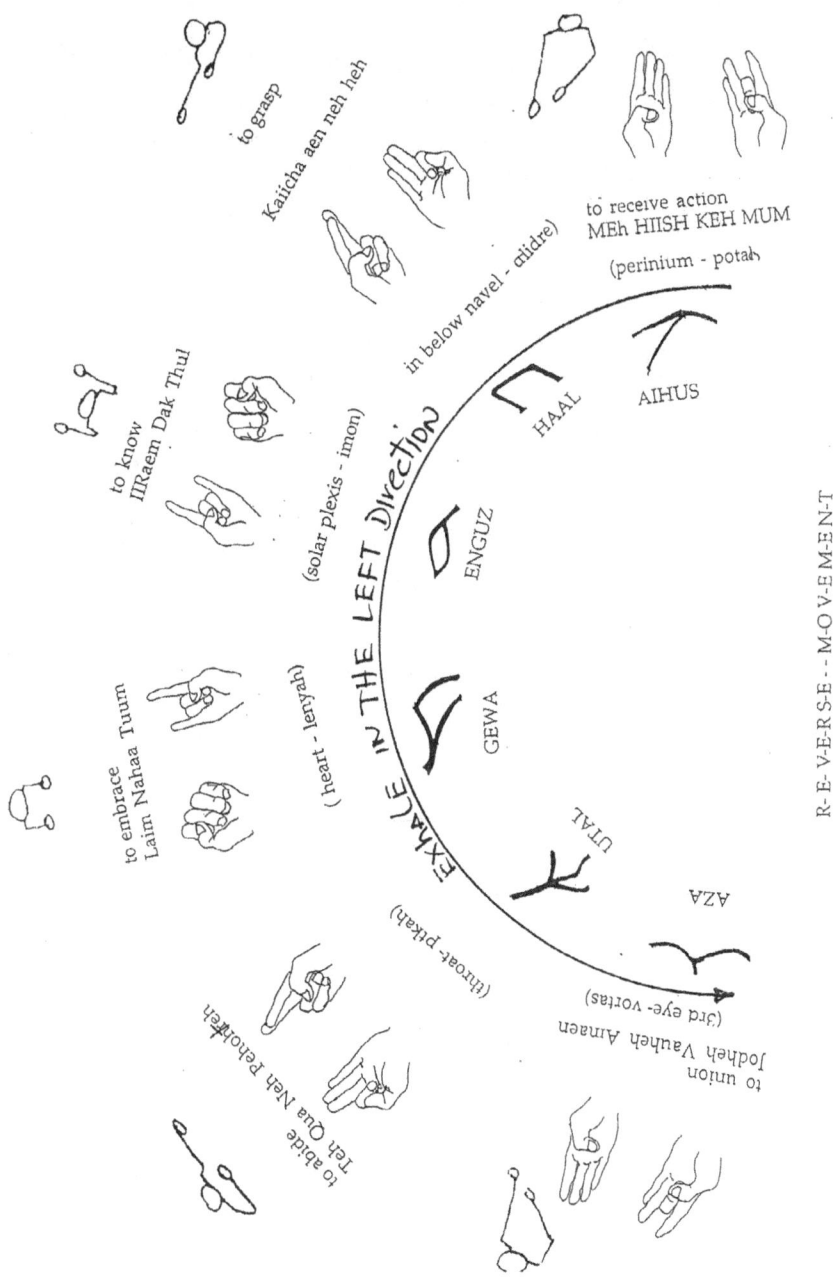

Rengmiatralaat Illustration # 35

Rengshalaat First Octave, The Animal Forms

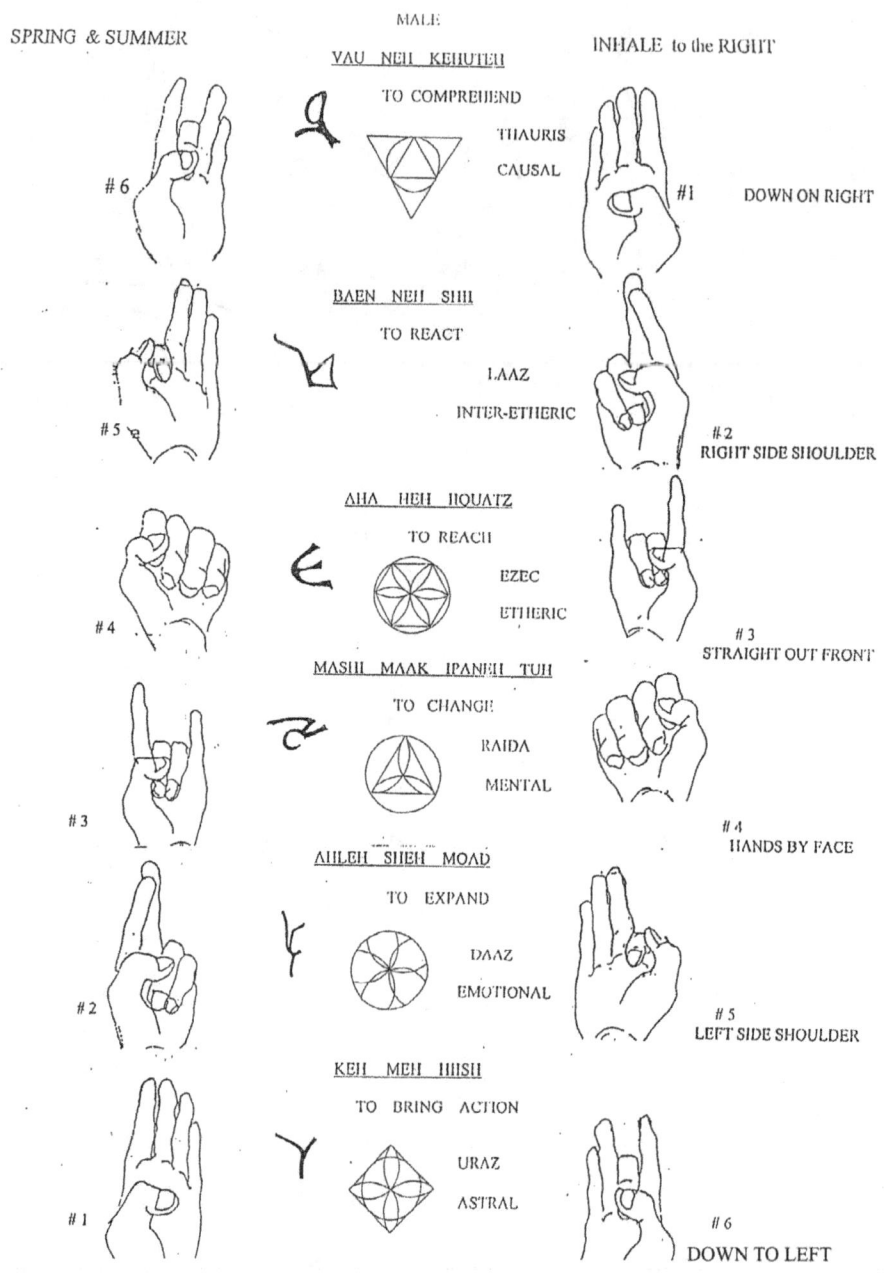

Rengmiatralaat Illustration # 36

Rengshalaat First Octave, The Animal Forms

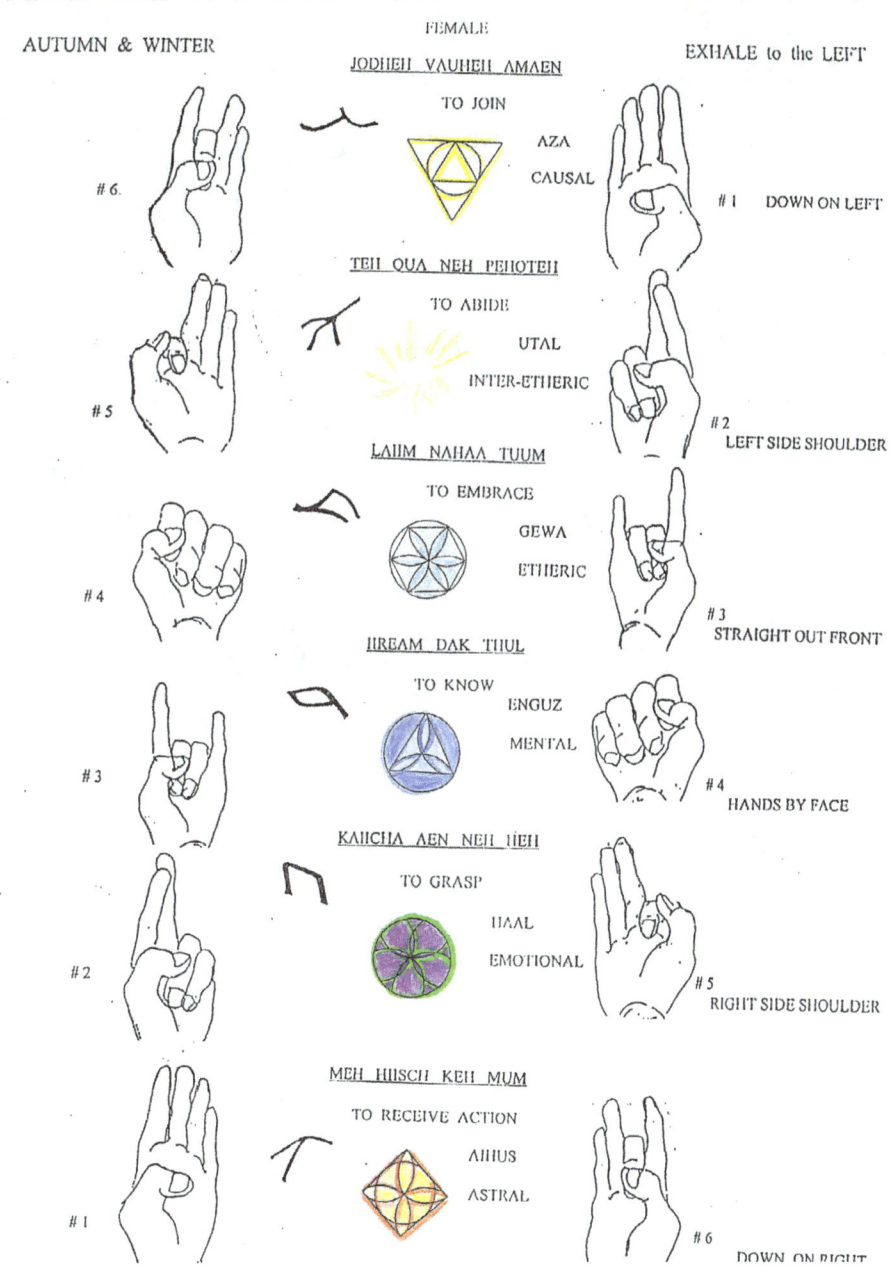

Rengmiatralaat Illustration # 37

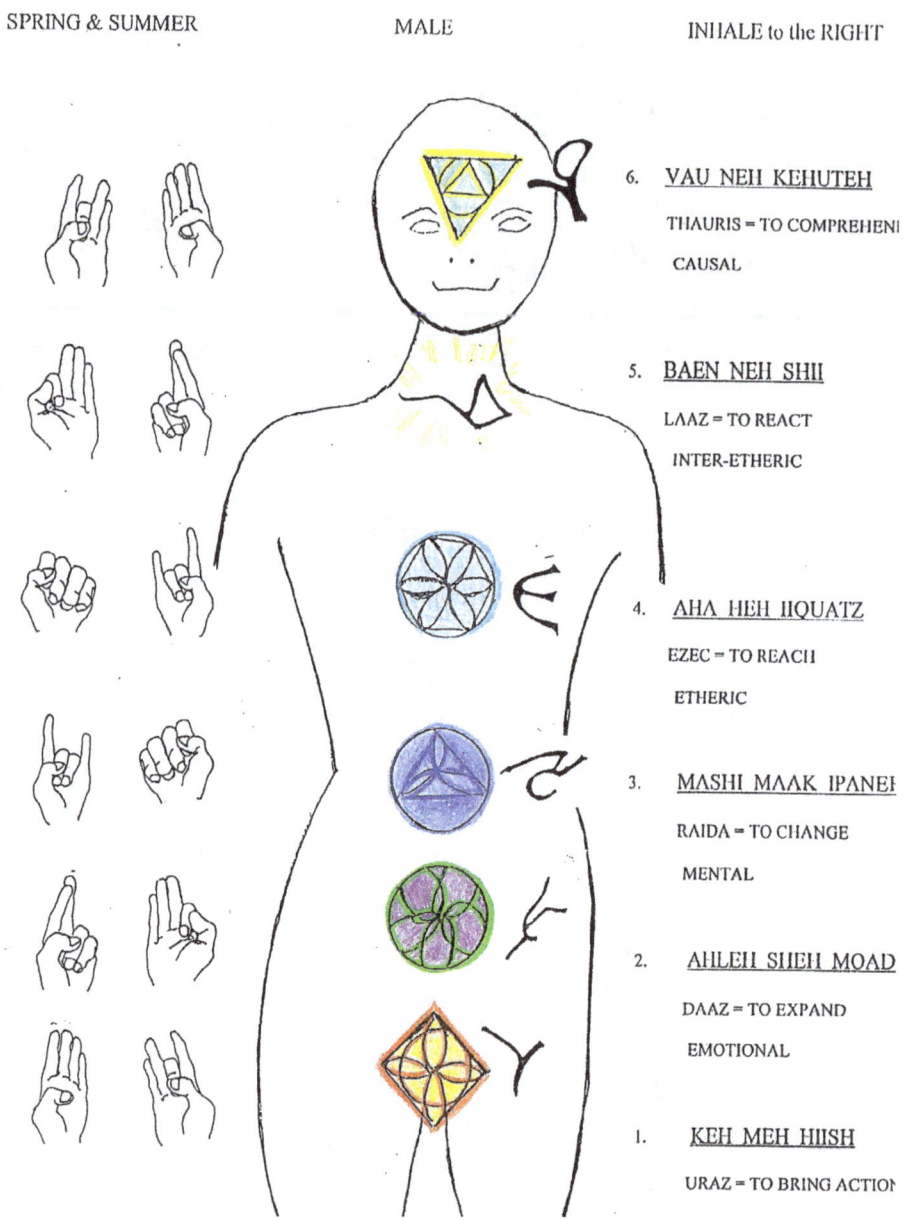

Rengmiatralaat Illustration # 38

Rengshalaat First Octave, The Animal Forms

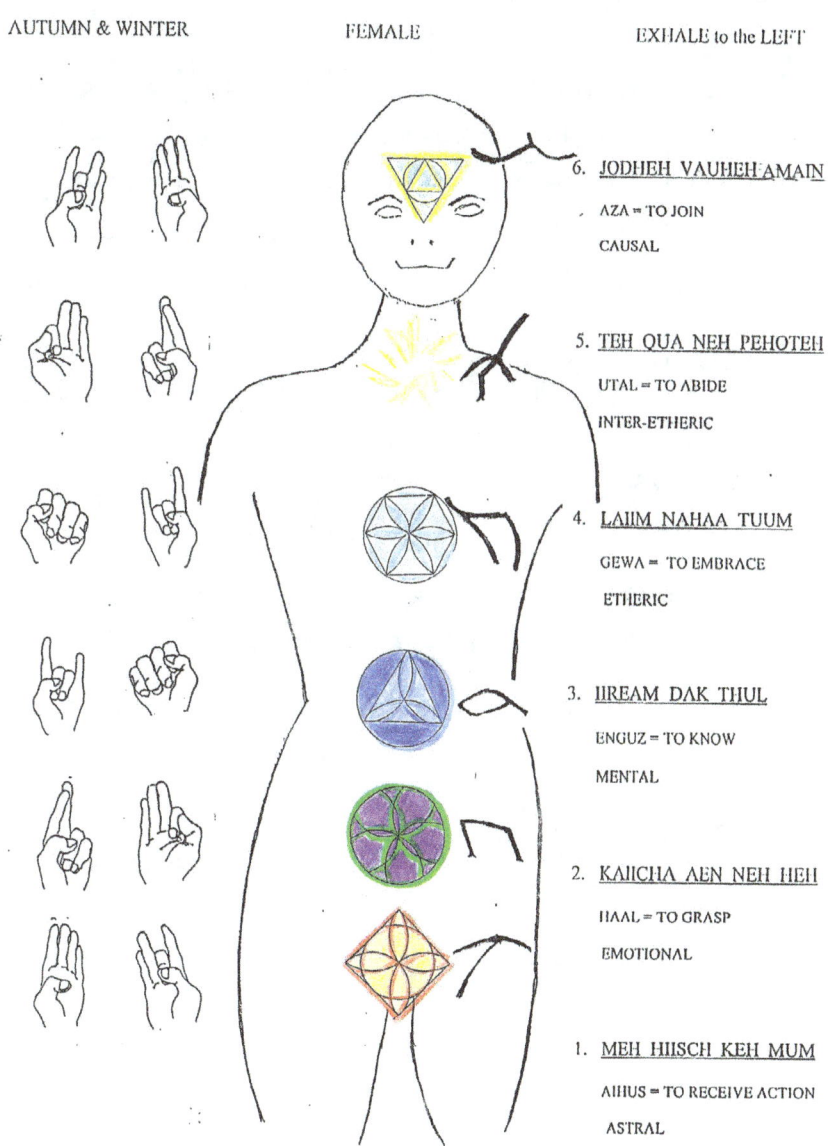

Rengmiatralaat Illustration # 39

SPRING TRIAD - LOWER TRIANGLE (MALE SIDE)

Each star pattern has a specific quality or essence that will affect you on a being level. In effect you are storing its essence in your Pukkas and directing it to your Subtle Bodies. It is necessary to combine the polarities to evoke the NEUTRAL.

1. **URAZ =** Male Action — TO BRING ACTION   Pukka: POTAH (PERINEUM)   Subtle Body: ASTRAL

2. **DAAZ =** Female Action — TO EXPAND   Pukka: DIIDRE (2" BELOW NAVEL)   Subtle Body: EMOTIONAL

3. **RAIDA =** Neutral — TO CHANGE   Pukka: IMAN (SOLAR PLEXUS)   Subtle Body: MENTAL

1. TO BRING ACTION (M) + 2. TO EXPAND (F) = 3. TO CHANGE (N)

SUMMER TRIAD - UPPER TRIANGLE (MALE SIDE)

1. **EZEC =** Male Action — TO REACH   Pukka: LENYAH (HEART)   Subtle Body: ETHERIC

2. **LAAZ =** Female Action — TO REACT   Pukka: PTKAH (THROAT)   Subtle Body: INTER-ETHERIC

3. **THAURIS =** Neutral — TO COMPREHEND   Pukka: VORTAS (3RD EYE)   Subtle Body: CAUSAL

1. TO REACH (M) + 2. TO REACT (F) = 3. TO COMPREHEND (N)

Rengmiatralaat Illustration # 40

AUTUMNAL TRIAD - LOWER TRIANGLE (FEMALE SIDE)

Each star pattern has a specific quality or essence that will affect you on a being level. In effect you are storing its essence in your Pukkas and directing it to your Subtle Bodies. It is necessary to combine the polarities to evoke the NEUTRAL.

1. AIHUS = <u>Male Action</u>   <u>Pukka</u>   <u>Subtle Body</u>
TO RECEIVE ACTION   POTAH   ASTRAL
(PERINEUM)

2. HAAL = <u>Female Action</u>   <u>Pukka</u>   <u>Subtle Body</u>
TO GRASP   DIIDRE   EMOTIONAL
(2" BELOW NAVEL)

3. ENGUZ = <u>Neutral</u>   <u>Pukka</u>   <u>Subtle Body</u>
TO KNOW   IMAN   MENTAL
(SOLAR PLEXUS)

1. TO RECEIVE ACTION (M) + 2. TO GRASP (F) = 3. TO KNOW (N)

WINTER TRIAD - UPPER TRIANGLE (FEMALE SIDE)

1. GEWA = <u>Male Action</u>   <u>Pukka</u>   <u>Subtle Body</u>
TO EMBRACE   LENYAH   ETHERIC
(HEART)

2. UTAL = <u>Female Action</u>   <u>Pukka</u>   <u>Subtle Body</u>
TO ABIDE (agree)   PTKAH   INTER-ETHERIC
(THROAT)

3. AZA = <u>Neutral</u>   <u>Pukka</u>   <u>Subtle Body</u>
COME TO UNION   VORTAS   CAUSAL
(3RD EYE)

1. TO EMBRACE (M) + 2. TO ABIDE (F) = 3. COME TO UNION (N)

Rengmiatralaat Illustration # 41

The Torax, Geometrical Alchemy

This practice is governing the alchemical laws of sacred geometry and the use of pure elements.

During World War II, the Germans were very close to creating the first atomic bomb. They had already completed their heavy-water experiments. In the US, scientists were concerned. They theorized the possibility but did not have a clue as to how to begin. An Italian alchemist explained the alchemical secret to convert base elements into sublime elements through pure elements and sacred geometry. In the early part of 1942, the first atomic pile was created under the direction of Dr. Enrico Fermi. A secret program called the Manhattan Project created a chain reactor under a Chicago squash court, proving the concept of atomic fission. The pile was made as a geometric structure utilizing pure elements of uranium and carbon. Later, a practical application of an implosion device using a sustained nuclear fission was created by Dr. Robert Oppenheimer and tested at Los Alamos, New Mexico. The rest is history.

This same sacred geometry is utilized in this spiritual work, to convert the base matter in the human body to a higher form through the process of a singularity of vibration of all the atoms, to vibrate at the same frequency. The singularity leads to a chain reaction of the energy in the tissues through the exchange of energy of the mitochondria.

Thus, the light body is created, leading to a transformation or ascension.

In this case, the Torax focuses first on purifying and harnessing the sexual force, while activating the inner will. This will serve to strengthen and empower the consciousness. It will free and transform the emotional energy and will untie the three knots of the heart: Greed, Pride, and Fear. Time and space are then lost. This enables the true perception of the relationship of heaven and earth to coexist in the moment. Then the real self emerges. The purpose is to awaken and lift up the dense physical matter and make it more conscious, just like awakening the elemental consciousness in the chain reaction of fission.

The first step or level of the Torax is to access the feelings and sexual force, to transform them together into pure elements and provide the fire for the first order of transmutation. The negative feelings are bound by sexual energy, and that prevents the penetration and neutralization, thus maintaining the cycle of permanent lower vibrations and limitations of physical existence.

The second level of the Torax deals with alchemically merging the transformed feelings with the etheric body aspects, thus opening the throat puuka and preparing the way for the Torax at level three, which involves the merging of the unified etheric body to the crown by merging the energies of the star patterns with the energies of the unified etheric body. This brings integration of all three and creates union and ascension.

The Torax, Geometrical Alchemy

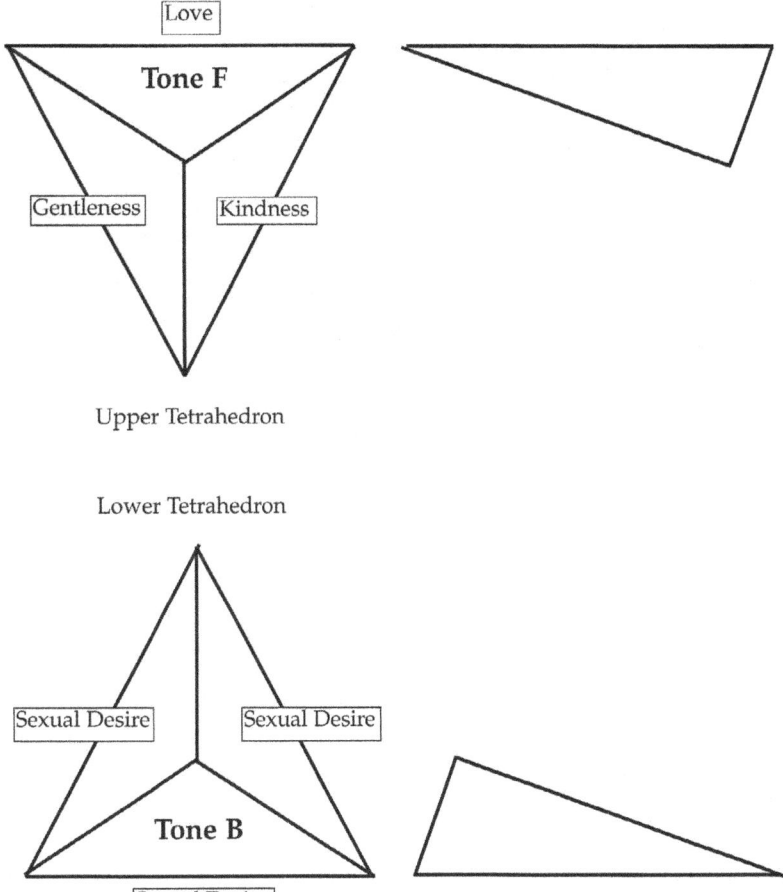

Torax Alchemical Meditation Level I

Torax, Geometrical Alchemy Illustration # 42

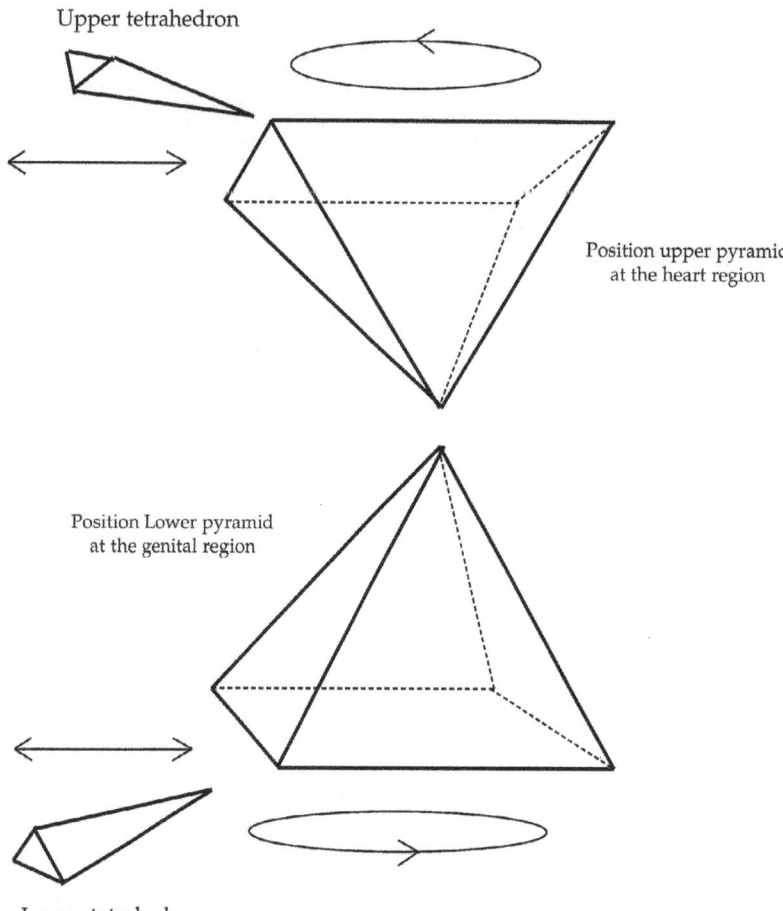

Torax ALchemical Meditation Level I

Torax, Geometrical Alchemy Illustration # 43

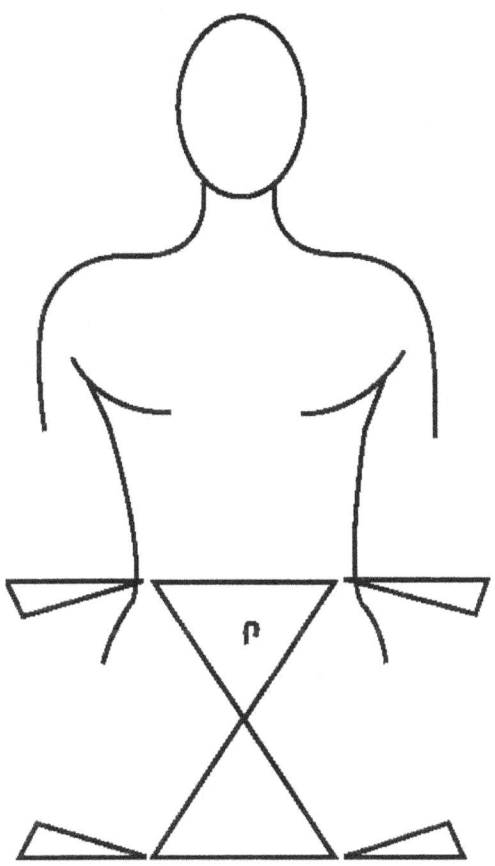

Torax, Geometrical Alchemy Illustration # 44

The Torax, Geometrical Alchemy 132

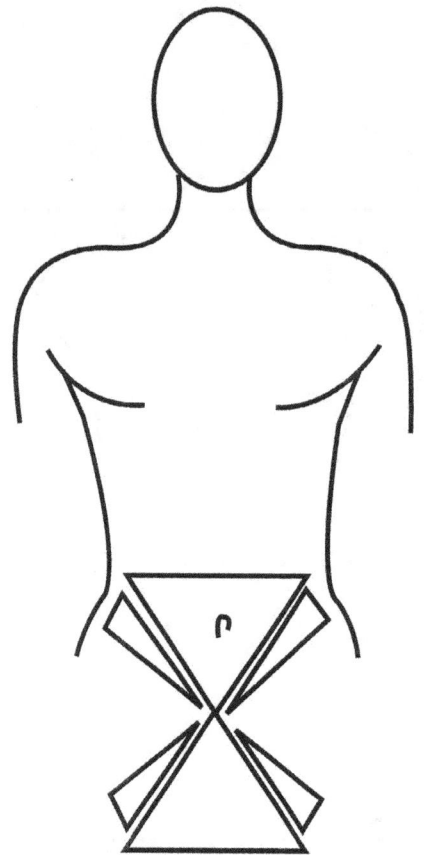

First Sphere of Influence

Torax, Geometrical Alchemy Illustration # 45

133   The Torax, Geometrical Alchemy

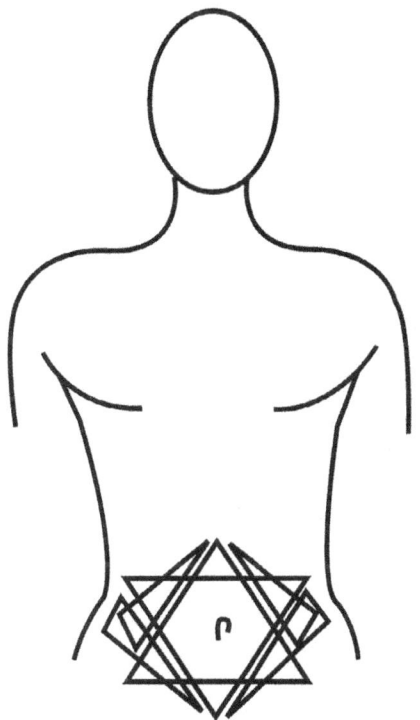

First Sphere of Influence

Torax, Geometrical Alchemy Illustration # 46

The Torax, Geometrical Alchemy 134

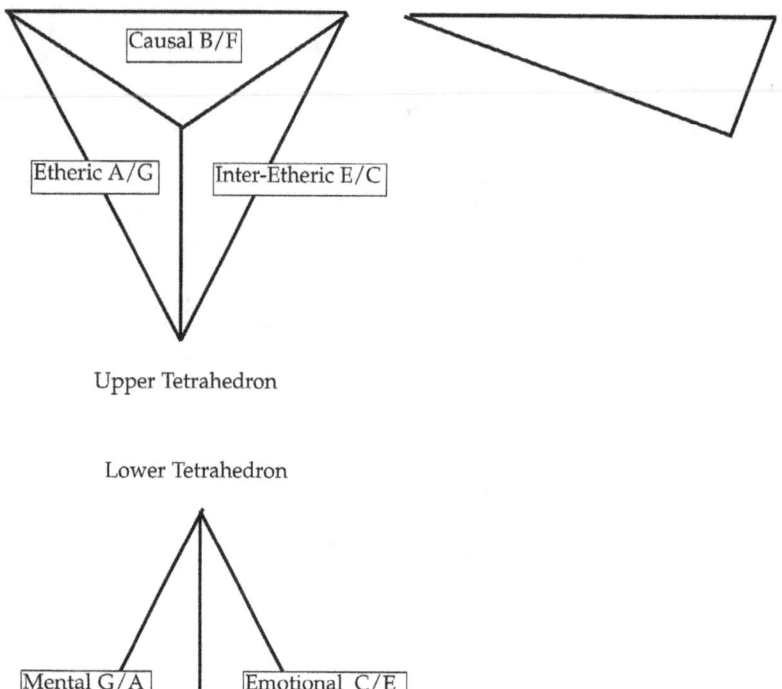

Upper Tetrahedron

Lower Tetrahedron

Torax Alchemical Meditation Level II

Torax, Geometrical Alchemy Illustration # 47

The Torax, Geometrical Alchemy

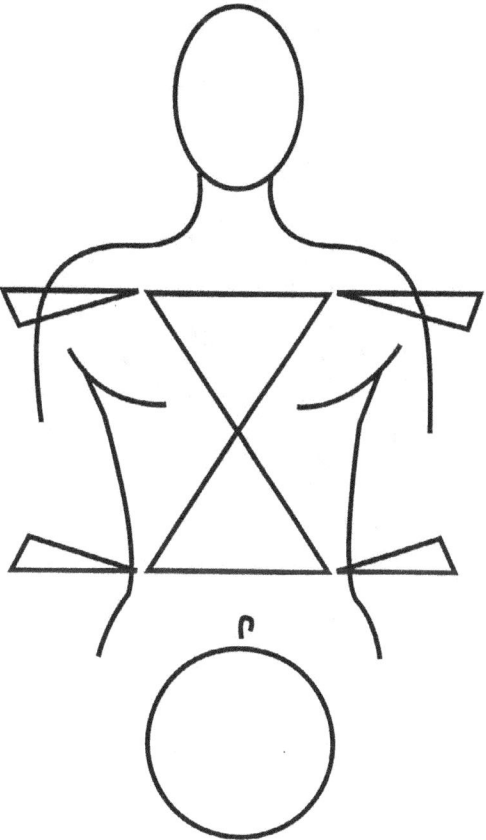

Torax, Geometrical Alchemy Illustration # 48

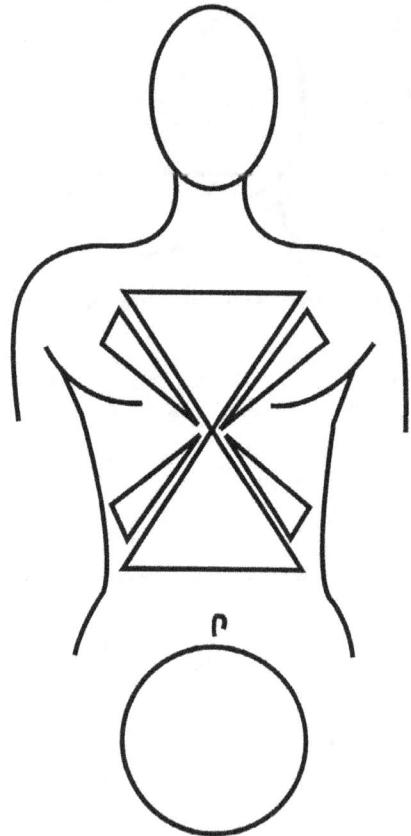

Torax, Geometrical Alchemy Illustration # 49

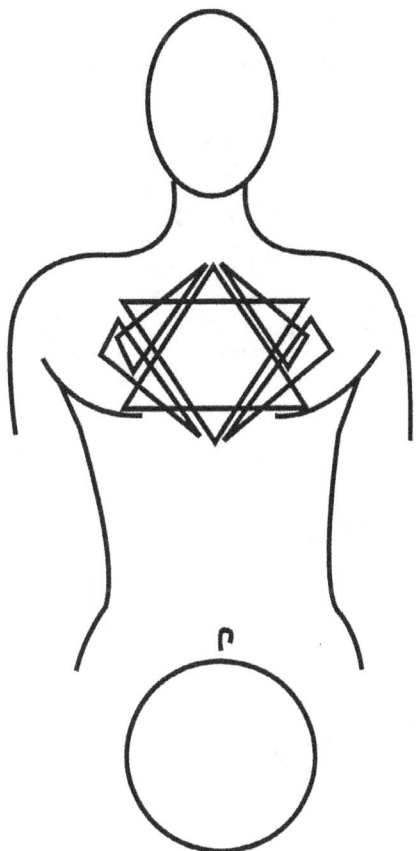

Torax, Geometrical Alchemy Illustration # 50

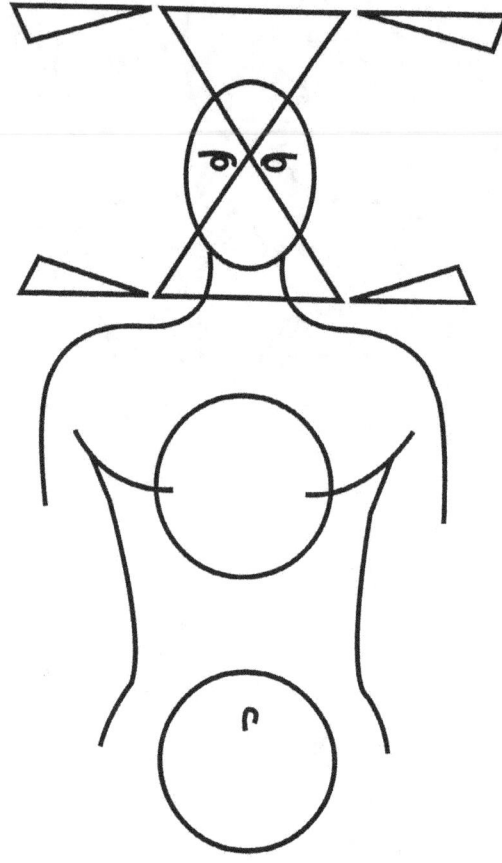

Torax, Geometrical Alchemy Illustration # 51

Torax Level III
Third Sphere of Influence

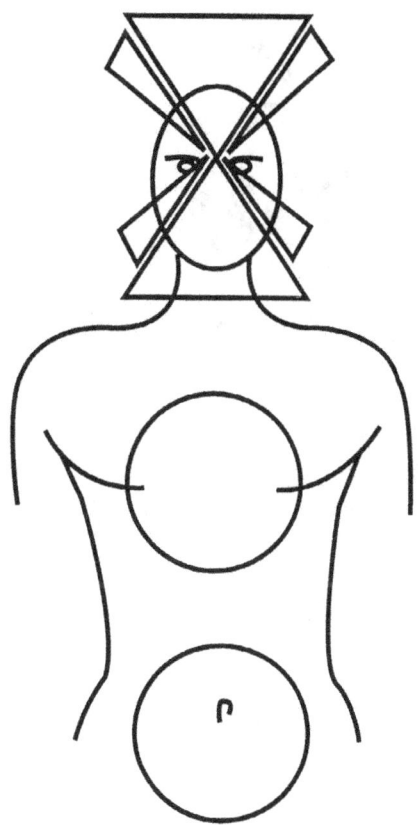

Torax, Geometrical Alchemy Illustration # 52

Torax Level III
Third Sphere of Influence

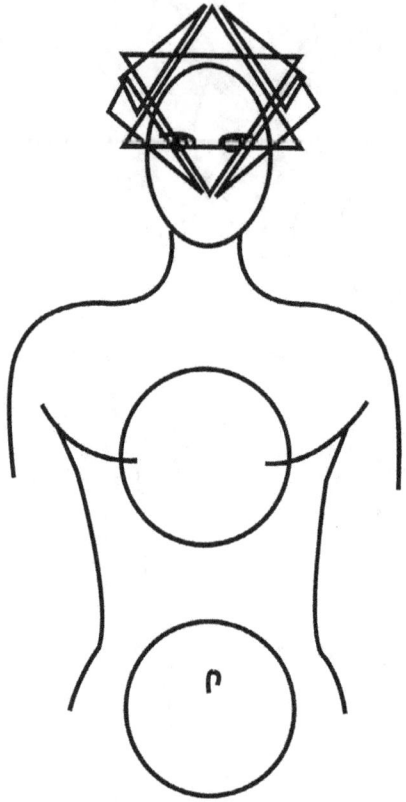

Torax, Geometrical Alchemy Illustration # 53

The Torax, Geometrical Alchemy

Torax Level III
Third Sphere of Influence

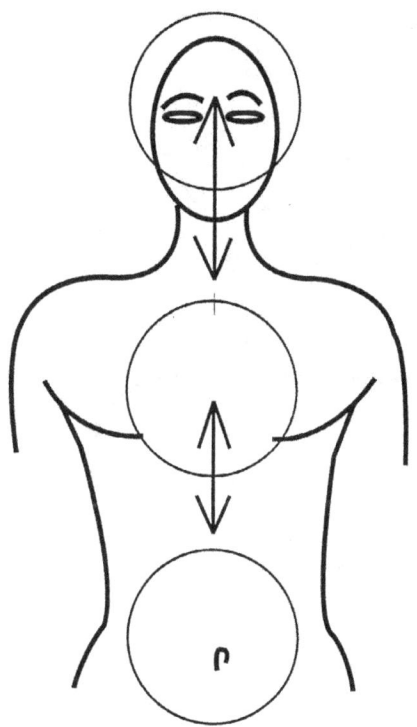

Torax, Geometrical Alchemy Illustration # 54

Torax, Geometrical Alchemy Illustration # 55

Torax Level III
Union

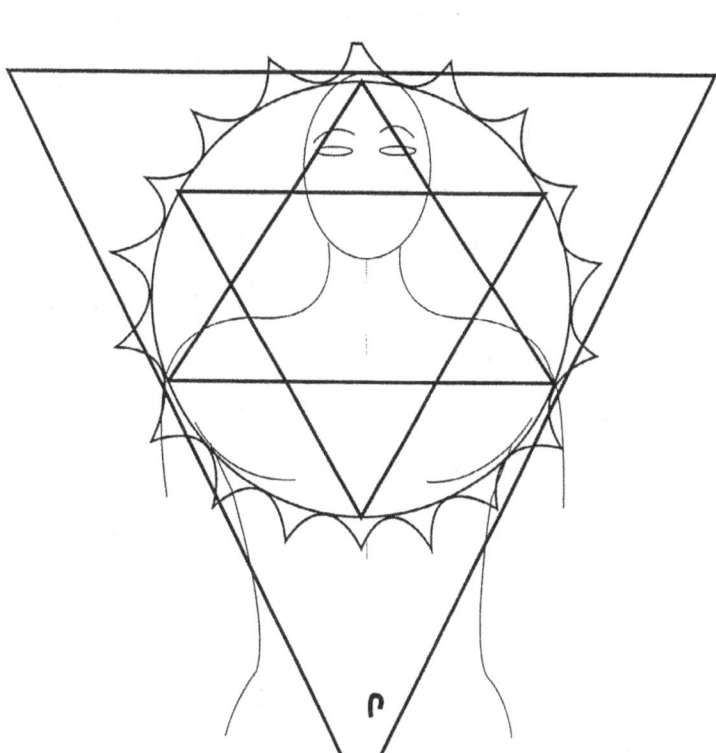

Torax, Geometrical Alchemy Illustration # 56

The Dragon's Breath

Nine Levels of the Dragon's Breath is done at night at dark (Note: Only candlelight can be used for light.) It is advised to keep a chart to keep track of the work.

The Dragon's Breath work culminates with the use of all the attributes of neophyte training: visualization, concentration, imagination and determination, patience and steadfastness. As one proceeds through all the levels, the energy is multiplied a thousandfold.

The practitioner is advised that it may take some years to reach the ninth level, and though the goal is clear, the ninth level is truly comparable to the Everest of training. Practically speaking, one could achieve the fifth level and be able to continue with the spiritual work throughout one's life without trying to go further. So, then it becomes a matter of being able to digest that amount of energy in the final analysis.

In time, usually after the third level, the stamina and strength limitations will become obvious as well. In this case, the practitioner must recognize those limitations and remain at the level the practitioner is able to manage and must not move on to the next level until a renewed sense of strength and energy is present.

The challenge to the practitioner will be obvious. In terms of endurance, it is equivalent to the Taumlec Arc. At the end of each practice session, the use of the ruler is expected and quite necessary. The bunching of energy where there are areas in the body that physical trauma has occurred and/or emotional trauma can still rest within the tissues unconsciously as a natural defense mechanism to protect the organism overall. It is in those areas where the aspirant must attend and focus to release those traumas by necessity.

After the fifth level of the work, a distinct trembling will occur first at the pelvic region and will move up into the abdomen and into the heart, using the will and mind to create a sense of peace and trust that the work is not becoming deleterious to the health of the body.

Level 1: Do these four exercises four times, sixteen sets (approx. 1 hour)
Exercise #1
Embracing the Dragon

Take a horse stance posture (standing with knees bent in a semi-squat as if sitting on a horse), hands at the waist level on each side, with palms up and sides of wrists facing the abdomen.

Begin "bellows" breath (rapid breaths at the abdomen) fifteen to twenty times inhaling/exhaling, ending with an exhale completely ending in a vacuum.

Focus the attention at the perineum without taking a breath. Still holding the vacuum, move the attention upward along the spine in the back, to the L5 position (gate of life-opposite the navel), still continuing to hold the vacuum, then move the attention onto the T11 mid-thoracic (behind the heart), still continuing to hold the vacuum. Move the attention to the rear seat of the skull (jade pillow at the nape of the neck), still continuing to hold the vacuum. Move the attention to the crown.

Continuing to hold the vacuum, then move the attention to the point between the eyebrows, then continue to hold the vacuum and move the attention down to the throat (making sure the tongue is at the roof of the mouth). Then continue to hold the vacuum and move the attention to the heart. Then continue to hold the vacuum and move the attention to the solar plexus. Continue to hold the attention and move the attention finally at the navel. Now the individual can take a breath. (Wait for the sensation of a worm wriggling in the pelvis-abdomen region.)

Slap the abdomen with both hands with the palms open, then move up to the chest. Then slap the arms and move down to the legs, first on the outer side, then switch to the inner side.

Now move to the top of the head and then behind the

head at the back of the neck, slapping with both hands while walking around several times. Return to the original position in the horse stance and return to slapping the abdomen several more times.

Then stomp the ground. With the arms swinging back and forth, hop off the ground with both feet two to three times, and land bending at the knees. (This is called grounding.)

Now return to the horse stance. Rock the upper part of the body at the waist back and forth from side to side, while exhaling with a grunting sound and immediately inhale quickly before shifting to the opposite side doing the same. Each side is one cycle. Do three cycles of this action.

Then shake the head quickly side to side several times, holding the tongue to the roof of the mouth while humming a high tone. Then shake the head slowly (half as quick) while humming a lower tone. Then walk around freely before going to the next exercise.

Exercise #2
Ruffling the Feathers of the Angels

Take a horse stance again. hands at the waist level. On each side, make fists clenched with palms up. Begin the bellows breath as in exercise 1, ending in a vacuum. Then inhale slowly while bringing the fists and arms forward, rotating the fists with the back of the hands facing each other.

Then, open the hands while making a wide, sweeping motion from the front and center of the abdomen around to the sides of the body while exhaling. Then make a short burst of inhale while bringing the open hands close to abdomen, fingers pointing toward the rib cage. Then raise the hands with fingers still spread open up a few inches. Do not exhale, but make another short burst of inhaling the breath.

Repeat, raising the fingers each time a little higher while taking another short burst of inhalation. Do this action two more times until hands and fingers are pointing to the upper chest on each side. Then rotate the palms facing away from the chest and push the hands out and away like claws and exhale.

Then bring all fingers and thumbs together on each hand, making a shape of a flamingo beak form, pressing them close together with some pressure.

Draw each beak up and back toward the chest, while at the same time taking short bursts of inhaled breath. Do this movement two more times, ending with the arms folded in front, hands in a beak form in the front of the chest like a praying mantis.

Then spread the fingers apart while still in front of the chest. Move palms facing downward toward the ground, while exhaling. When hands are at the waist, rotate the palms away from the body, while leaning forward and still exhaling. Stretch out the tongue, make a hahhhh sound with the throat while exhaling the rest of the air into a complete vacuum. Hold for thirty to sixty seconds until the sensation of a worm turns or wiggles in the region of the pelvis and abdomen. Note: If the head is at the right angle, the heartbeat will be heard loudly in the inner ear. As the vacuum continues, the heartbeat will slow until it stops. (Note: The heart hasn't stopped literally, but it means time has stopped for the practitioner.)

Now return to the horse stance and repeat the slapping, stomping, and rocking the body side to side while rapidly breathing to each side and humming while shaking the head as in the first exercise.

Exercise #3
The Turtle

Take the horse stance again. Then bend over at the waist with the upper torso positioned between the bent legs. The head will be facing the floor. The back is kept flat like a table parallel to the floor. The hands are clenched as fists with the palms up under the chest, with forearms close together and between the knees, with the elbows suspended clear of the legs.

Begin to inhale rapidly from the abdomen, similar to the bellows breath. The abdomen will expand to each side in this position, breathing as a buffalo would breathe. Take ten to fifteen breaths, and then exhale all of the air and enter into a vacuum for thirty to sixty seconds until the worm turns. Then drop the hands with fingers loose, pointing to the floor. Look up and face forward while breathing normally. Follow this with the slapping, stomping, shaking, and humming as before.

Exercise #4
Grasping the Tree

Take a horse stance, knees bent, arms out front, elbows bent and relaxed, palms facing inward, thumbs out, and other fingers in.

Bellows breathe fifteen to twenty times, then exhale into a vacuum approximately thirty to sixty seconds until the worm turns.

Slap the abdomen, chest, arms, and legs, top of the head, and back of the neck three times. Stomp the ground and do the grounding. Then do the rocking back and forth, from side to side while breathing in and out.

   Then shake the head quickly holding tongue to roof of mouth while making the high tone, then shake the head slowly, making a lower tone. Walk around freely for a few minutes. This last movement should be followed by the practice of the ruler, combing out the energy.

The following is the set pattern for the sequence of these exercises:

Level 1: single combination of 4 exercises x 4 at 16 sets (1 hr.)

Level 2: double the above exercises, making it 32 sets (2 hrs.)

Level 3: triple the above exercises, making it 48 sets (3 hrs.)

Level 4: quadruple the above exercises, making it 64 sets (4 hrs.)

Level 5: quintuple the above exercises, making it 80 sets (5 hrs.)

Level 6: sextuple the above exercises, making it 96 sets (6 hrs.)

Level 7: septuple the above exercises, making it 108 sets (7 hrs.)

Level 8: octuple the above exercises, making it 124 sets

(8 hrs.)

Level 9: nonuple the above exercises, making it 140 sets (9 hrs.)

    This then completes the dragon's breath preparation. Level 9 should be done three times per week thereafter, for a minimum of nine weeks in a row. However, if this series of nine weeks is broken up in any way, the practitioner must start over for another nine weeks.

    If, however, the practitioner is successful, then the practitioner has completed this work, never having to repeat it again.

Sound Power, Mantras

The power of sound was well known among many cultures for thousands of years. Of the five senses, the use of hearing when danger is near has been a staple of humankind's survival since the earliest time. The faculty of hearing was primary to all life forms seeking safety. Humans were no different. Their entire existence depended on cleverness in dealing with nature and predators. The beating of sticks together making loud and threatening sounds could drive predators away or even herd them into traps for capture.

The sound of thunder, earthquakes, and volcanic eruptions, along with thunderstorms and meteor strikes, continued to ravage the land day and night. This kept humans in a constant state of fear for their lives. If that weren't enough, large predators roaming about looking for their next meal signaled their arrival by their heavy weight stomping and shaking the ground they walked on. Hearing those sounds gave cause to run for the nearest cave or climb to a high limb of a tree to escape ferocious jaws of death.

As the environment settled over time and the larger monsters were gone, successful hunting of smaller game depended upon the control of sound by keeping quiet while approaching close to prey, increasing the probability of success with their weapons while using animal skins like moccasins to soften the sound of their footsteps.

The use of skins stretched over open logs as well as hollowed out logs used for drums played while singing loudly instilled courage to engage in fighting and would help to keep predators away from camps at night. Later, those same drums were used to signal to others through a rudimentary form of coded messages over long distances.

Hollowed-out tree limbs were also fabricated to function as primitive instruments to play musical tones, such as the flute. Tones were made by blowing air over a small hole like a whistle, or by blowing air across the end of a larger tube, making continuous very low tones, such as the digeridoo by aboriginal tribes.

These instruments became a useful adjunct to the adulation offered to the gods for fertility, crop growth, help for herd migration, and basic needs for psyche survival and comfort through spiritual ceremonies involving the rite of passage into manhood, or sacred shamanic ceremonies to enter trancelike states to commune with the gods. Also, the voice is used to offer homage to deities, such as in the Muslim mosques for calls to prayer.

Through many millennia, these sound-making techniques continued to evolve into more sophisticated instruments, using strings bowed or plucked as on an erhu or rebab in Middle Eastern countries, or struck and strummed with the fingers, which produced very complex and beautiful sounds that could ease tensions, creating peaceful environments conducive to meditational states, such as with the sitar in India or the shamisen in Japan.

In the modern world, more sophisticated electronic instruments allow for making and recording of artificial sounds or sounds in nature or recording those who are skilled at playing these instruments, which can be used to support the creation of peaceful environments in the home for entertainment and meditation.

Holy men or monks are often making unusual sounds uttered singularly or in groups, making a chanting pattern, to induce a deep meditative state of mind. These unusual sounds are utilized in such a way as to create resonance within the body and within the ventricles of the brain. The brain has seven ventricles that wind through the cerebral hemispheres. When stimulated, can cause interactions inside the brain that alter brain functioning related to certain frequencies.

These frequencies have been mapped and are known to define certain mental states. These range from Beta frequencies (fifteen to thirty cycles per second), Alpha frequencies (seven to fifteen cycles per second), Theta frequencies (four to seven cycles per second) and Delta frequencies (one to four cycles per second).

Beta states are defined by states of hyper-awareness felt through daily activities. The Alpha state is that condition of relaxation felt just before going to sleep. The Theta state is very often attributed to discovery, such as an "aha" moment in the solution of a problem. The lowest state is Delta, which is reached at the deepest level of sleep (usually connected with REM, which means rapid eye movement occurring while dreaming).

Another important quality of sound is when it appears at both ears simultaneously but at different rhythmic patterns. These sounds are referred to as binaural sounds. The mind may be operating at a slightly elevated mental state, for example, at fifteen cycles per second during the day.

A unique property of the brain is it can synchronize different sounds in each ear in order to pinpoint their location of origin, but more interestingly, these properties can be used to trick the mind to lowering its own brain state. Importing two sounds that differ by the frequency desired, such as fifteen cycles of sound in one ear while at the other ear receives eight cycles of sound. Given several minutes of time past, the brain tries to synchronize the two sounds and creates a third tone, which is the harmonic or difference tone. This is called heterodyning.

The effect of heterodyning is the mind will lower its frequency to the difference tone through a natural process of homeostasis or balance, resulting in a change of brain state from medium Beta to medium Alpha, creating greater relaxation for the whole body.

When monks enter a cave to meditate, they will utter mantra sounds that are binary in nature, such as from the Sanskrit language. The sounds coming from the monk's voice will bounce off the cave walls as an echo. It will arrive at a different time to the sound of the monk's voice heard around his head. This can create a slight heterodyne effect and can change the monk's brain state to a deeper relaxed state or meditative condition.

The use of brainwave synchronization as a spiritual tool, becomes important and can circumvent the need for years of practice by the simple application of this technology.

The neurons in the brain are electrical impulses and are subject to visual stimulus, auditory stimulus, and magnetic stimulus. Each of these sensory inputs affects different areas of the brain and even different sides (left and right hemispheres).

One of the drawbacks imposed by alien intervention

with human development is the bifurcated brain (the creation of two hemispheres). This was imposed to restrict evolutionary development. If one chooses to use this kind of technology, where the photonic stimulation, auditory stimulation, and magnetic-field stimulation is used electronically with a heterodyning approach, vastly improved progress with achieving profound spiritual awakening can occur with greater effect by establishing whole-brain synchronization in this way.

In addition, if the ancient Sanskrit language (mantra utterances) is utilized, that relates to the stimulation of the puukas. The nervous system development becomes greatly enhanced toward spiritual evolution.

The puukas, or energy windows, are similar in relationship to the spinal cord as the ventricles in the brain are related to the endocrine glands, meaning here the pituitary, pineal, hippocampus, amygdala, and thymus.

Without the additional help of this technology, the possibility is quite small the aspirant will achieve the desired goals. The Mantras that form the trigger sounds to awaken the Puukas from the base to the crown are: Bam, Lam, Ram, Wo-am, Eram, Shiram, and Aum. These can be spoken aloud or silently with lips parted, but with certain phonetic Vril intonation: Beh-Ah-Meh, Leh-Ah-Meh,

Reh-Ah-Meh, Wha-Oh-Ah-Meh, Ee-Reh-Ah-Heh-Meh, Shi-Heh-Reh-Ah-Meh, Ah-Oo-Meh. There are other secret deeper resonant but heterodyned sounds that stimulate and awaken the Puukas into an evolutionary state.

Logically, one might conclude that the right approach is a linear approach to spiritual work. This is not true, and the ancient sages and magi discovered this long ago.

This truth is revealed in the symbolism of the Anneagram and the Star of David. It is interesting to note that the Jewish people chose to use the six-pointed star as the symbol of the Jewish Nation of Israel. On the surface, the six-pointed star represents the king and his rule of the tribe of Judah. The esoteric meaning is quite different. It represents the secret spiritual path as set down in the great temple in regard to the right path of ascension of the human to heaven.

The star represents physical actions and is apparent, but it does not reveal the secret teachings. This is made apparent by the secrets of the Talmud. In the Talmud is revealed another level of understanding that indicates the six obvious points of physical action, but beneath this outer canon there is another symbol called the Anneagram. In the Anneagram, there are three additional components that are not obvious, represented by the silent triangle, a divine mathematical composition of 3-6-9.

This harmonic arrangement only arises when the other movements are understood. The subtle bodies arose from the divine quantum after the fall. The fall, those elements or parts of the Most High separated from full understanding of the Quantum. These isolated components of consciousness developed in a descending order of de-evolution from the first cause (be-cause) or causal body, the first separation. With each degradation of consciousness away from the Most High, there arose the etheric, emotional, and finally mental body.

, The mental body defined the emergence of a separate ego mind and the ultimate defiance of the fallen to declare by the fallen, they would and could function in reality without the guidance of the One and thus make their own reality, believing they did not need the oversight and union. After the separate will emerged, the final degradation developed into the Astral, or Astral body. After that emerged and then the end result, a manifestation of the physical illusion of reality.

The way back is more convoluted. The way to return was not going to be easy. The path follows the sequence of 1 (unity) divided by 7, the subtle body subcomponents, or .142857, the pattern illustrated by the ancient Anneagram. Further complicating the path of ascension is the use of the shadow tonalities or heterodyned tonal qualities that represent the divided subtle bodies.

Their true vibration is a shadow or ghost frequency

developed by the sacred Lamdoma, a pyramidal symbol indicating the correct tonal mixtures to arrive at the rising fourths and the descending fifths mixed together.

The tones cannot be generated straight forward but must be derived by the consciousness indirectly. Those secret spiritual tonalities were removed from sacred music by the church in Rome to keep the masses from rising above the priesthood cult. The monks of the Orthodox Church sang these frequencies in their devotional music to recreate these binaural frequencies, only acquired through the diatonic scale, which was switched by the church to the "adjusted scale" of modern music. Now modern music does not have the power it once did in the Middle Ages to inspire toward higher realms. Recordings with the sacred binaural tones must be used to promote the alignment and awakening of the subtle bodies. See illustrations.

Note:

It is important that the aspirant creates a recording of binaural tones on a device such as an MP3 player so that the phantom tones of the six subtle bodies can be heard. Those six pairs of tones are recorded separately on a stereo track opposing ascending fourths to descending fifths to create the phantom beat frequences.

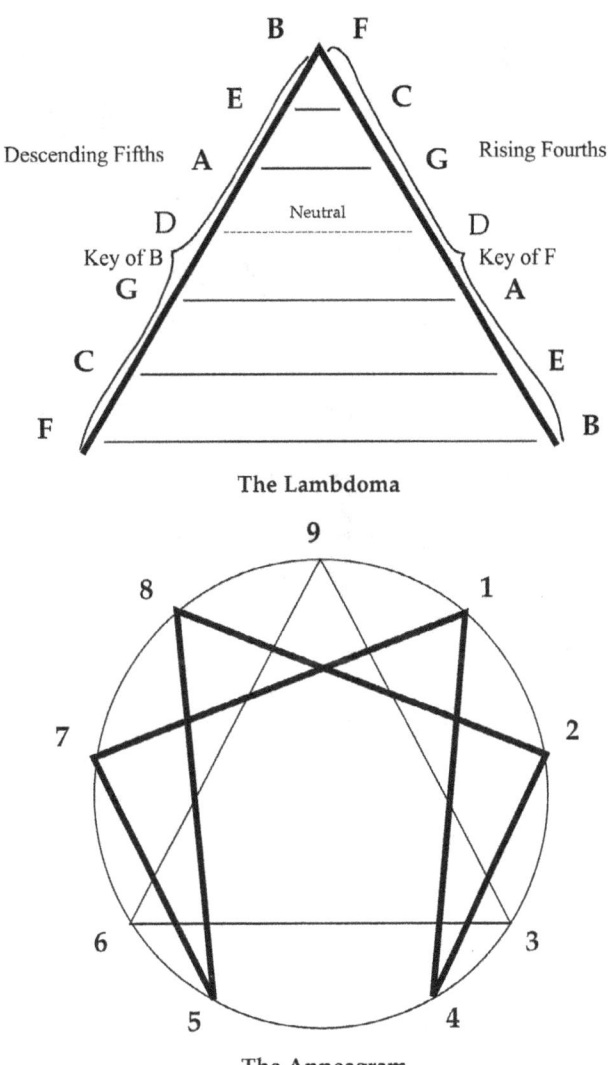

Fourths and Fifths, Anneagram Illustration # 57

Fourths and Fifths, The Anneagram

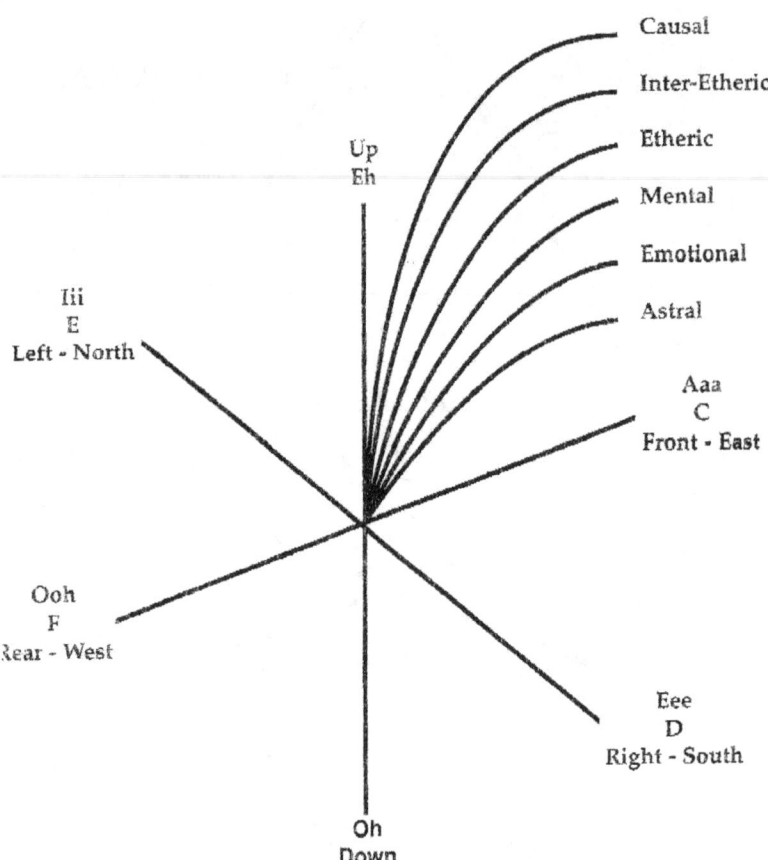

Fourths and Fifths, Anneagram Illustration # 58

Fourths and Fifths, The Anneagram

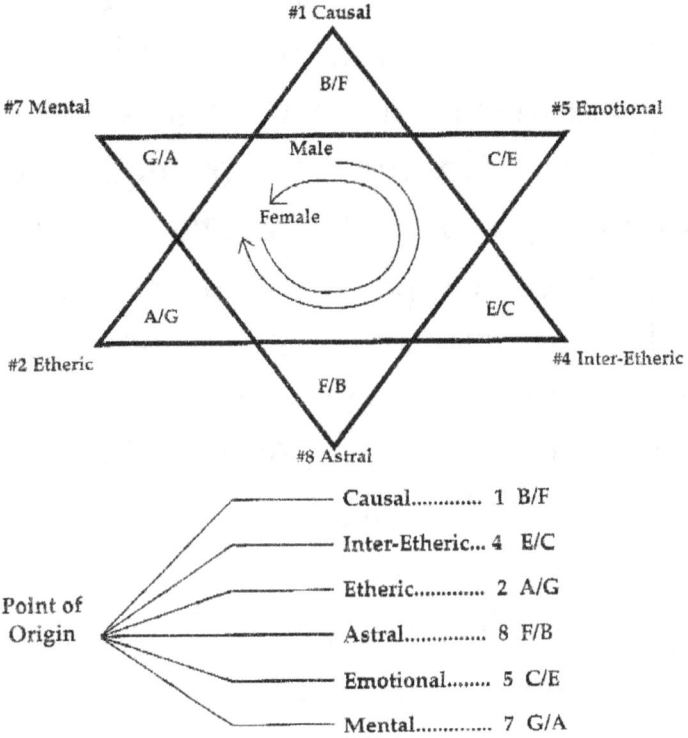

Star of David - Anneagram
Sequence

Fourths and Fifths, Anneagram Illustration # 59

Other Dimensions, The Quantum

As we grow into adulthood in the West, we are taught in elementary school about the three dimensions—length, width, and height. In three-dimensional space, otherwise known as the Cartesian coordinate system, plotting a point in space requires six points with lines drawn between them. Then to plot a destination from that point is a seventh point.

A theoretical fourth dimension was suggested by Albert Einstein involving a point traveling through time. The Einstein-Rosen bridge suggests a bridge that could exist as a "wormhole" between two points in space that circumvents the time involved to cross the planes of both dimensions. In effect, a short circuit of time and space.

In recent years, the concept of combining time and space is the subject of discussion among physicists called "space-time." This refers to the idea that space can be a medium where distortion of space itself can occur, an idea advanced by Einstein to describe the elemental force of gravity as a distortion of space by a body in space in time. Distortion of space-time can be made to circumvent the laws of physics to where the speed of light can be violated.

Physicists have proposed that there are more dimensions in the universe than the three-dimensional universe we have come to know and understand. They have come to this conclusion due to the mathematical proposition that they can exist. The exact nature of these other dimensions is a matter of conjecture and debate. One of the most popular descriptions of other dimensions is something called string theory, which suggests at least ten dimensions exist in all.

From a spiritual point of view, there are seven dimensions. These are not an empirical physical set of dimensions as such, but from the idea of wave mechanics or wave theory of reality, these are dimensions separated by frequency.

As Einstein tried to prove mathematically, there was the possibility of a unified field theory defining a set of forces all agreeing that could adequately describe reality. He never accomplished that feat. The underlying purpose of all this research was to establish proof of the origin and purpose of existence.

The innate problem is that realization of the multiverse is and can only be observed subjectively through the evolution of consciousness. That means that the true nature of reality is defined by a number of levels of consciousness that are differentiated by frequency. So, to perceive a different dimension, one needs to raise one's vibration of consciousness to recognize a particular dimension.

The fundamental structure of consciousness is divided

by six levels, with the seventh level directly relating to the quantum itself. The goal of all spiritual systems is to reach the ultimate realization, which is the quantum. So, what is the quantum, exactly?

In most religions, there are presented only two basic dimensions, the physical realm and the spiritual realm or heaven. Where the spiritual realm exists also exists the angels, the demons and the ultimate creator of all things, God.

The concept of an anthropomorphic view (a human view of God) as an old man sitting on a throne overseeing all life everywhere and sitting in judgment against all life everywhere with a definite set of moral values applied.

Here the promise of everlasting life after exuding from the mortal coil is based upon the successful adherence to those moral values, otherwise punishment is in the offing, where the soul is sent to hell, another dimension of eternal damnation and suffering.

Unfortunately, the average person is not equipped to deal with the truth of the reality of being emotionally because of the superstitions and mythology in which religion is based, created by the few to control the many, and also to provide a mechanism for civil behavior in a society.

The simple truth is, there is no God per se, even though

"those on high observed the heavens and earth" (the actual translation of the beginning words in Hebrew of Genesis) as opposed to the incorrect translation, "God created the heavens and the earth." This declaration could still refer to aliens who came from the heavens to earth. As the Sumerian cuneiforms suggest when they describe the Annunaki, "Those from heaven came down." And they made man in their own image, through DNA interference to further along the advancement of life.

Perhaps a more definitive way to describe the prime mover or quantum is a way of being that is harmonious, peaceful, and omniscient. Others who are present in the multiverse who may be millions of years ahead of us mere humans on the evolutionary scale, are the "new kids on the block"; the rest are demigods as such, simply because of their understanding and advanced knowledge. Advanced scientific knowledge can easily appear as pure magic to the ignorant.

Astral Travel

Astral travel means that the consciousness actually leaves the physical body and is able to go to remote or nearby places and be aware of those locations as if being there physically.

This has happened to some people who are under duress or emotionally depressed. The more common experience is to find oneself floating slightly above the body without any prior indication this is happening, which can be a shocking experience and often leads an individual to think they have died and are apart. There are times that someone has been apart during sleep, and when they awaken, they cannot move for some minutes until they have completely returned.

The fact is, this experience is more likely to occur while asleep and dreaming. The author believes that everyone leaves the body at night. But what is actually happening?

The human being possesses a number of "subtle bodies," not all of which are actually physical. Each body is relegated to a particular dimension by virtue of the vibration of that dimension.

The strong belief is that the physical body is certainly real enough because of our five senses that give the sensation of reality as it is known. Even the physical body is not solid, per se, meaning it is a complex combination of electromagnetic waves making up the "matter" that describes the tissue, blood, and bones, condensing into the shape we call the body.

The philosophical component involving the exact nature of awareness that gives consciousness within the body is still eluding scientific investigation. Upon death, it is known that the weight of the body drops slightly at the point of departure of the consciousness. So, what is leaving exactly, and where does it go? These are age-old questions that are usually left at the doorstep of religious responsibility.

Depending upon what religious denomination is speaking, they all have their idea as to what happens. In this context, esoteric spiritual systems have long since offered another explanation about the nature of consciousness and how it functions. In this case, the Atlanteans brought this subject into clear focus at a later time in their development.

That became a serious point and fundamental underpinning of their understanding of spiritual work and the purpose of spiritual training beyond the aspects of devotion to a deity.

The astral component in the definition of travel refers to the astral body, a subtle body nearest to the physical body, and actually appears as a body double if seen apart by others.

As in the case of Jeshua (the true name of Jesus), who was reported to be seen in many places at once teaching large groups of people. Also, this attribute called bilocation allowed him to avoid capture many times during his ministry.

In spiritual work, there are three stages of spiritual separation: remote viewing, astral travel, and teleportation. The first is stage is simply the mind viewing a remote location and being able to report the activity and details of that location without leaving the body.

The second stage is where the astral body actually separates (with a sensation of leaving physically and feeling the sudden loss of body weight) with a complete awareness of moving around and through physical objects such as doors and walls, even rooftops. While in that state, individuals can look upon themselves and see a replica of themselves but with a distinct bluish and ghostlike appearance. They are not hampered by the physical laws of gravity and inertia, so flight is also quite common, even beyond the planet. Breathing an atmosphere is not required, so traveling in outer space is also possible.

There are two vibrational conditions that the astral body can exhibit. It can vibrate very close to the vibration of the physical body, and that is the normal condition throughout the day while fully awake. The second vibrational state is when the astral body can vibrate at a higher frequency nearer the frequency of the astral component of the quantum, allowing it to pass through objects.

Under certain conditions, the astral body could leave the physical body and still be near the vibration of the physical body. In this case, the astral body would need to open doors and not be able to pass through walls or fly.

When the astral body leaves the physical body at night, it will move on into the astral kingdom, a dimension of the Quantum and returns in the morning as the individual begins to awaken.

Very often, if the mind remains conscious for a time at the point of the body going to sleep, it will move along with the astral until the mind gets caught in the imagery of a dream, but sometimes what is visualized is the artifacts of what the astral body sees or experiences in the astral. There is no time in the higher dimensions. So, sometimes the snippets of what is seen could be precognitive, offering glimpses into the future or the past for the mind to comprehend.

The most desirable way an astral body can leave is from the brow, but sometimes it can also fall away from the solar plexus area. In some of the rarer cases, one can leave through the feet, but this often brings a host of unpleasant experiences. Though it is desirable to leave from the front of the body, very often the astral can drop out of the body from behind. When this happens, the individual needs to be prepared for the sudden drop as if falling for a few moments.

In the earlier stages of this practice, the individual needs to remember keep the eyes open, otherwise black is all that will be seen in the experience.

The primary requirement for successful practice is that the mind remains awake while the body is asleep. It is recommended that a short nap is taken before an individual attempts separation; if not, exhaustion of the physical body will surely overtake the attempt, and the individual will simply fall asleep in the process.

Remote Viewing

This skill is naturally acquired but can also be developed. In the early 1970s, the US government Defense Intelligence Agency discovered the Soviets spending sixty million rubles on research into something called psychotronics. The Russians were deeply involved with developing agents that had psychic skills, for the sole purpose of psychic espionage. This was called "remote viewing."

Secretly, in an answer to that threat by the Soviets, the United States began a program to accelerate that development in selected soldiers, utilizing unique psychoactive drugs such as LSD, mescaline, and other harmaline-based drugs under a program called MK-Ultra. It was a disaster. The program was abruptly halted by Senate investigations.

Then in 1972, a new approach was taken at the Stanford Research Institute with an investigation into extrasensory perception, and specifically, remote viewing was investigated. Research developed by two physicists, Dr. Russel Targ and Dr. Harold Puthoff at the Institute attracted the interest of the US Army at Fort Meade, Maryland.

People were tested both from the military and the civilian sectors using techniques developed by Dr. J. B. Rhine at Duke University to determine a predilection toward psychic abilities. Under the leadership of Ingo Swann, the army began the Stargate Project in 1978. A small group of candidates showing promise were introduced to an advanced training program based on that training protocol under the CIA called SCANATE (Scan by Coordinates). This was the beginning of the successful secret US psychic espionage program as an answer to the Soviet threat. Remote viewing is a natural part of spiritual abilities when the consciousness is awakened.

Remote viewing is a form of clairvoyance and/or clairaudience, the ability to psychically perceive information at a distant location and at a different time, such as the future. It was known to exist for thousands of years, long before the US Army discovered the ability. First, they had to get past the conservative skepticism prevalent in the military.

The approach to developing this skill is simple. The basic idea is to quiet the mind, then begin to mentally focus and reach out to a target. In the case of the military approach, the idea of a target was a set of desired coordinates, targets they wanted specific information about.

In the spiritual approach, it's more about expanding the student's senses beyond the body and reaching toward a known location, already familiar to the student, relating to previous experience of the location. One could say this practice is a prelude to astral projection, the act of projecting the subtle light body to a remote location.

In principle, there are three stages of this remote witness activity: first, remote viewing without projection, then projection of the light body and finally, teleportation, the dematerialization of the physical body, projecting the consciousness and physical counterpart to a distant location and then rematerialization.

This idea stretches the imagination into the realm of the unreal and perhapsscience fiction. It has happened, as reported by witnesses, on rare occasions to some individuals spontaneously, but usually under emotional duress.

Sometimes it can happen with the accidental emergence of a portal (or doorway). Such was the case reported by the FBI once in the late 1980s. A woman and her son stumbled upon a doorway appearing in their living room one day on the East Coast. The mother saw her son enter the doorway and disappear. She ran after him, only to find herself suddenly some three thousand miles away on the streets of San Francisco in her nightgown. The case was quickly closed by the FBI. Later, it was reported by Charles Forte, in his book of strange occurrences entitled The Fortean Falls.

Portals are a natural phenomenon that occur in the fabric of spacetime, as riffs or tears appear in the fabric of a dimension, and a brief Eistein-Rosen bridge occurs between this dimension and another. If one enters such a doorway, there is no telling where or when they might end up. The fact is that hundreds of thousands of people disappear every year without a trace.

Lucid-Dream Control

Everyone dreams at some time during their sleep. Some dream in color, while others dream in black and white. This effect reveals a certain lack of focus and more, a lack of engagement in the dream sequence. The one who dreams in color may be more engaged than the one who dreams in black and white.

Many people do not remember their dreams and claim that they do not dream. Dreaming is a necessity in order to clear out unresolved issues from the day. The mind is first and foremost an organizer. It abhors loose ends, so to speak.

Using a computer analogy, dangling feelings and unspoken reactions to circumstances, such as silent frustrations over situations or perhaps minor altercations, are zero data. This fragmented information must be repackaged and placed in a mental "box" and removed from the consciousness for the purposes of the preservation of the system. On the mental, emotional, and psychological levels, balance must be maintained. This is another form of innate homeostasis.

If this activity did not occur, ultimately mental illness would be the end result. Even what are referred to as nightmares are useful, even though they can be quite frightening. The idea that experiencing a nightmare is far superior to leaving these dangling "demons" hanging around is hard to accept or believe.

If a nightmare continues to repeat, then it becomes a cry for help on the unconscious level, to warn the individual an issue needs to be dealt with on the outer level of conscious behavior, and psychiatric care is suggested.

Dreaming can also be healing in nature and can make a huge difference in a situation where circumstances are difficult on the outer conscious level, and therefore compensation occurs and is necessary on the inner level. Both of these conditions fall under an automatic response and are believed to be outside of a person's normal range of control.

Dreaming is still considered an autonomic response and beyond volitional control. In the early 1970s, the concept of biofeedback was introduced, whereby a person could actually indirectly control certain biological processes believed to be beyond their control, such as blood pressure and heart rate.

By focusing consciously on creating a tone, which is generated by electronic apparatus detecting heart rate and blood pressure when reaching a safe range, the individual can form a loop or feedback process to indirectly access those otherwise unreachable body processes. Hence the term biofeedback represents a way to reach the stability of those body processes.

Later, biofeedback was replaced with augmented control of brain states with something called brain synchronization. Using bifurcated sounds or binaural sounds, as pulses supplied through earphones underneath the level of hearing, when added to a pleasant musical track can force the brain to enter a more relaxed state.

Brainwaves have been mapped by neuroscientists defining four basic states of awareness. These waves are divided by frequency, such as the Beta state represented by a range of frequencies between fifteen and thirty cycles per second. The Alpha state is represented by a range of frequencies of seven to fifteen cycles per second. The third lower state is Theta, which is represented by a range of frequencies of four to seven cycles per second. Finally, the lowest state is Delta, which is represented by a range of frequencies of one to four cycles per second.

Beta is characterized by normal waking activity involving thinking about coordinating activities throughout the day. Alpha state is characterized by a relaxed state that occurs just before going to sleep. Alpha is a state that calms the nerves, slows the heart rate, and lowers the blood pressure.

The Theta state has been characterized by what is called

a problem-solving state. While mapping the brain activity, an individual may be working to resolve an issue or come to an answer to a question, resulting in what is called an "aha" moment. That insight or discovery gives rise to a feeling of exhilaration, and at that moment, the Theta frequency is said to occur.

The Delta state occurs during the night, when deep sleep is reached. It usually lasts only for about an hour. This state is recognized and associated with REM or rapid eye movement during sleep. This also signifies when one is in the process of dreaming. Not much is known about the purpose of Delta.

The use of binaural tones, tones at two different frequencies, played simultaneously in the left and right ears, can induce some of these states through the process of heterodyning. This is the process of mixing two tones to create a third beat or difference tone, such as when a fifteen-cycle tone is played in the left ear and an eight-cycle tone is played in the right ear; a third different beat is heard that is at seven cycles per second.

This third phantom beat heard is created by the mind trying to synchronize or organize a disturbing difference in the two inputs.

The discovery of this mental effect causes the mind to

lock on to and synchronize with the third or beat frequency. This results in forcing the mind to change its own brainwave frequency to match, thus restoring homeostasis or balance.

If the tones are heard audibly, the effect is diminished over time as the mind will ultimately give up and shut out the disturbing beat frequency.

So, if the binaural frequency is placed on a stereo track that has a volume below the threshold of normal hearing, masked by another set of sounds such as pleasing music, the mind will focus on the louder sounds heard and ignore the underlying beat frequency. Then the synchronizing effect will continue, causing the mind to slowly match the beat frequency, unaware of the subtle impact.

This means that the individual has only to listen to both tracks to achieve a more relaxed state in only a matter of fifteen to twenty minutes, without the need to focus on creating the effect themselves. The caveat here is, the track of binaural beats cannot be abrupt but must be slowly ramped down over a few minutes, otherwise the sudden changes of brain state can create a headache.

So, biofeedback has given way to brain synchronization as a more effective way to control some of the body processes. Some enterprising developers have tried to use this technique to enhance learning new skills by applying subconscious messages along with the binaural tones. The results are not as effective as they may proclaim in all cases.

In addition, others have tried to use hypnotic subliminal suggestions with binaural technology to actualize changes in behavior or feelings overcoming patterns of negative behavior from childhood traumas or stressful situations, such as posttraumatic stress conditions from warriors returning from life-threatening battle conditions. These techniques are not ironclad solutions and can vary with each individual.

Lucid dreaming is an unusual state where the individual is experiencing a dream sequence that is every bit as real as the waking state experience. The realness is defined by experiencing at least three of the five senses vividly, such as physical touch, sight, and hearing. All five senses could be engaged as well, such as taste and smell.

If the dream sequence is pleasant, then it becomes desirable to experience it with as much vividness as is humanly possible. There are techniques suggested here to augment the successful attainment of lucidity. Applying the techniques of brain synchronization of the two hemispheres on a regular basis can greatly increase the possibility of lucid dreaming to occur.

In this case, the Alpha is the most desirable state. Then later, one could induce the Theta state as well, if one wanted to help the process of accelerated learning and/or problem solving. Special memory techniques are sometimes effective in triggering the lucid state.

Exercise #1
Before going to sleep at night, tie a brightly colored string around the wrist and gaze upon it several times in the day. While gazing upon the band, associate the band with becoming aware of your surroundings, such as a car passing by or noticing someone with an attractive appearance or something unusual in shape. Then, when preparing to sleep, make a mental note to look for the band on the wrist when you are beginning the dream.

If you can discover the band, then find a mirror and look at yourself in the mirror and say hello to yourself. Lucidity will engage. Then the individual will cease being a pair of floating eyeballs just witnessing the situation and become actively involved, with most of the senses operating fully.

Exercise #2.
Make up an object in your imagination; draw it on a piece of paper. Take it up and stare at it many times throughout the day. Draw something unusual that would catch your

attention immediately, such as a blue rabbit with black spots or stripes. It can be anything, but it must be really out of the ordinary, not viewed in everyday life.

When you retire to sleep, make a mental note to the self to look for the unusual object or thing you were visualizing during the day. When you find the object, follow the instructions above to engage the rest of your senses.

Lucidity while dreaming can also lead to further skills while dreaming. When an individual is having a wonderful dream and they are awakened, a sense of loss is felt because of the belief that dreaming is accidental and a lost dream can never be recovered. This is not true!

With lucidity reoccurring over time, if a lucid dream is interrupted by a loud sound or needing to go to the bathroom at night, an individual can return to their bed, enter the lucid dream again, and continue where they left off. Nothing has to be given up or lost.

The Plasma Ball, Signs of Progress

Normally, a spiritual master offers constant assistance when teaching a neophyte or beginner. One of the unique properties of that close relationship is the specter of progress a student needs in order to realize the goal.

The modern concept of spiritual development is founded on a misconception. Modern belief proclaims that enlightenment is the goal. What does that mean exactly? If you ask fifty teachers, you might have fifty different answers to that question. The truth is, this idea tries to advocate one sudden burst of awareness. This idea is not only not true but unrealistic.

Real development comes from concerted effort persevering on a daily basis, with very small signs of progress along the way over a long time. Self-realization, meaning the discovery of the nature of oneself, is the real foundation of spiritual work. So, perhaps the best way to put it is development is not sudden but slow and tedious. The work may take an indeterminate period of time, or it may move along swiftly. It depends on the student and the information provided.

Those who would attempt to teach esoteric techniques now are often basing their techniques on false premises, erroneous information that is missing important pieces of the puzzle, or the information is wholly inaccurate. Also, the all-important aspect of detecting progress is missing because those who are attempting to teach esoteric knowledge are lacking the personal experience of success. It's all about making a living, making money on the ignorant.

For example, one Taoist master might offer the first alchemical meditation formula for $150, whereas another Taoist master may charge thirty-two ounces of gold. This is a striking comparison. It generates potential suspicion in the student about the moral character of the teacher in either case.

Though surprising, this comparison still does not represent a good way to determine if you are studying nonsense or the genuine article. That is why results are the only way of determining genuine information and by personal experience. So, false teachers cannot realize the important signs that a student needs to know.
Changes will occur in the student along the way that indicate progress.

The spiritual law is an old alchemical axiom: "as above, so below," but there is more to it. The complete statement is "As above, so below; as below, so it is above; and as it is inside, so it is outside; and as it is outside, so it is inside." This means in truth, all is connected.

If the student is successful working with higher unseen

energies, it follows there must be changes accordingly inside the physical body. The physical is but illusion; there is no physical body!

Changes in strength, stamina, acute awareness, clearer thinking, better memory, and recall of details are just a few. Old habits will fall away and will be replaced by new, more beneficial ways the student will have. Old antagonisms between members of the family will tend to dissolve, and the manner of behavior in social situations will change as well.

At a certain level, the auric field that surrounds the body will begin to purify and radiate a healthy glow. Very often, that glow is quite noticeable by others, noting perhaps through their remarks, such as, "that person looks really good for their age," or "that person is easy to talk to and is quite pleasurable."

Mood swings and the ability to handle stress are improved over time. Food cravings considered unhealthy would fall away in favor of more healthy consumption, such as organic food sources. The elimination of harsh lower-vibrational elements, such as smoking tobacco, or the consumption of strong alcoholic beverages, or drug abuse and even addiction could be eliminated.

After a time, the work will begin to reveal internal signs. One such sign is the flashing bright-blue light inside the inner eye when external lights are switched on or off rapidly or abruptly.

Also, the emergence of a soft blue sphere at the brow level inside the head with a display of plasma-like discharges dances within the sphere (see illustration). Certain pure auditory tones will be heard inside the inner ear, either on the left or right side, lasting for five to fifteen seconds or longer, indicating the nervous system is being retuned. (Note: This is not tinnitus.)

The need for less sleep will also become apparent. Also, the sudden appearance of starlike flashes in a room above or near others, while at the same time, vague colors may also appear briefly around certain people, perhaps when they are passionate or upset or greatly elated.

In time, more sophisticated effects may occur, such as spontaneous remote viewing of other locations, now or in the future. The realization that you are hearing the thoughts of others can also spontaneously occur. Out-of-body experiences can also begin to happen, perhaps when the student goes to bed. Also, lucid dreaming, where vivid details of a scene will be in brilliant color, accompanied by smells and visceral touching of objects and meeting other people the student may not know.

Placing the fingertips close together from each hand

and experiencing the energy flowing out between the fingers of each hand with a sense of real pressure from the energy can be felt.

There can be a sense of tingling at the crown, creating an intense desire to scratch the scalp, as well as a tickling sensation at the throat, likened to thousands of ants crawling inside. The urge is to cough, but the student should try to resist that urge and try to consciously keep the throat open until the tickling gives way to a strong wave of heat that rushes to the top of the head, leaving a slight dizzy sensation briefly after.

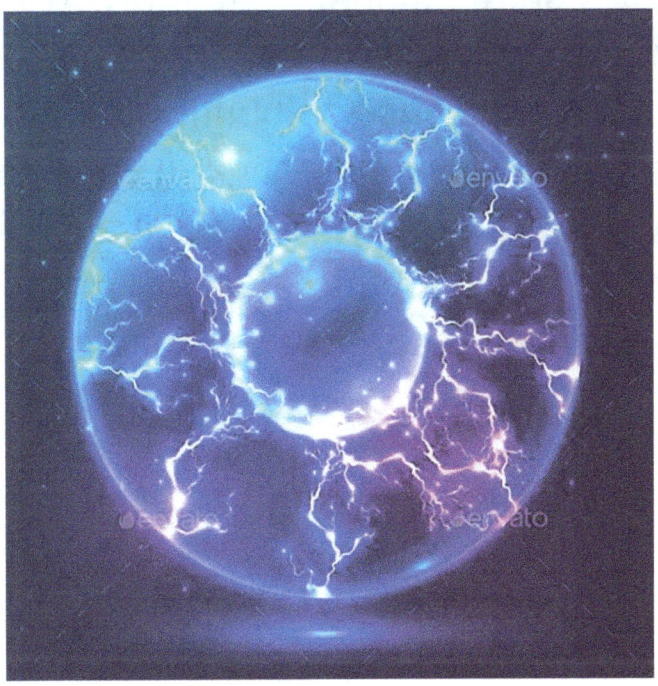

Plasma ball as seen internally Illustration # 60

Epilogue

This spiritual system is unique, and with the aid of this manual and the tools recommended (see illustrations), can be a rewarding experience. Since it depends on the particular lifestyle of an individual, the time devoted to the work is highly subjective and totally at the discretion of the practitioner.

This work does not require any sort of monastic lifestyle, and in the beginning of the practice, the requirements personally are more or less minimal. Later, as the work progresses, the individual will naturally gravitate to a more intense practice regimen.

As with any spiritual practice that involves meditation, concentration, and physical exercise, the work may seem daunting at first, but practice will build stamina and good traits in the aspirant's behavior that will enhance the experience within the work as well as family life where applicable and solid work ethics that will make for a smoother experience in the work environment.

Tools Needed for the Work

1. The Prism.

Working with the prism takes some getting used to with finding the best angle to hold it relative to the angle of the sun. Note: bright sunny days are best for vivid and strong colors. (Remember to adhere to the clock-viewing technique).

CAUTION:

Do not exceed more than fifteen minutes of exposure in any given week. This practice requires patience and does not work well with undue ambition to increase exposure, when there is a limit imposed by the body and the eyes.

2. The Beads.

There are two bead sets needed, one to count Arcs and one to count the four quadrants in the grand circle.

The Arc counter requires a string of beads, sixty count at each quadrant (preferably made of rosewood or similar) with four quadrants. Stone or jeweled beads are too heavy to use for any length of time. Because of the weight of the jewel or stone beads, the risk of the thread breaking is high. It is recommended that a spool of thirty-pound nylon fishing cord be used for stringing.

It is also recommended that the nylon cord be tied off at

the end of each quadrant, which will help the grand circle string to remain close together, avoiding too much separation, which makes it difficult to pull beads through the index finger and thumb easily. The size of these should be .315" in diameter (or 8 mm). The total number required for the grand circle string is 240 count. Each bead in the string should be separated by one magnetic hematite bead (6-mm diameter rondelle shape) and these can be obtained from eBay online.

The practitioner needs to also find four large unusual-shaped beads, as an example: one square, one round, one oval shaped, and finally, the primary starting bead should be a large seed bead 15–20 mm in size (see illustration) such as a Sibucau seed. Form a group of crochet threads of several colors approximately six inches in length and tied together in the middle then attached to the first bead. This signals the completion of one complete path around the grand circle and the beginning of the next round. Note: All of these wooden beads can be obtained from the Beads and Pieces company online.

3. The Ruler

The use of the ruler is important to smooth out the energy that can collect in various parts of the body, such as the arms, legs, and chest. Follow the directions given in the illustrations, which is done after all of the other energetic work is done for the day.

Construction of the deluxe ruler is a bit more complicated and may need to be done by someone skilled with materials and construction. The detailed drawings are itemized. Sources for the wood can be obtained from Amazon (called a "body back wood roller"). The roller needs to be cut in half and drilled through on each piece to accommodate the magnetic pole pieces that meet the thread steel rod in the middle.

The ball in the middle connecting the two wood pieces is made of magnetic hematite about two inches or 50 mm in diameter and also needs to be drilled to accommodate a steel threaded rod that fits into metal nuts. Round nickel end plates are needed (made at a machine shop) to complete the magnetic circuit. (See diagram.) The deluxe model is an adaptation of the Atlantean ruler that had Auriculum material in the middle, which is not available anywhere in the world now.

Note: For those who are not inclined to spend the money and effort to make the deluxe ruler, the original whole wood roller will conduct chi energy sufficiently to help smooth out the energy bunching that arises in the work and is also available from Amazon as the Body Back Roller.

Paanterah Kal-Circle of the Golden Shadow, Circle Walking
The aspirant can obtain a DVD of this movement that combines Agogik and Magogik energy in a slow circular walk. The DVD that best demonstrates this movement is done by a Teacher of Tai Chi. "Bagua Fundamentals" #SQ6574719 $20.95 From the HSing I Martial Arts Institute.

The Concentration and Visualization Ball
(Uxcell juggling ball) 1.18 inches (30 mm) in diameter; clear acrylic ball, obtained from Amazon
Whole-Brain Synchronization
Involves the use of an apparatus designed to provide light pulses, or sound pulses and/or magnetic pulses which are all binaural in their application at the resonance of the Earth, which is at 7.8 cycles per second.
Note: The aspirant can obtain prepared sound recordings needed for the work
from a seven-CD set in a package called the Hemi-Sync "Monroe Gateway Program" on Amazon.
Another resource is light and sound machines at Tools for Wellness online.

Tools Needed for the Work

Deluxe magnetic Roller Illustration # 61

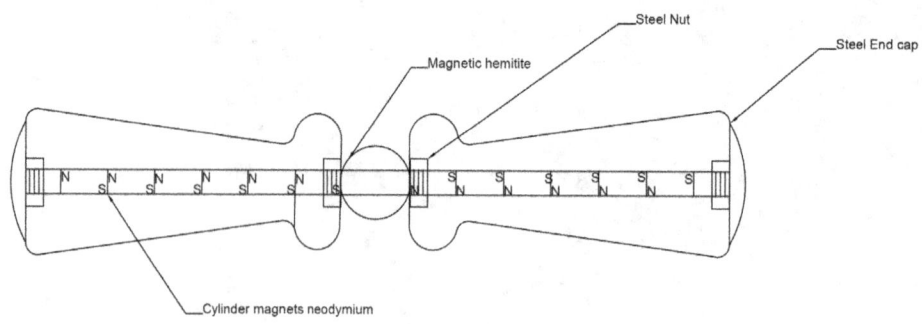

Deluxe Magnetic Ruler Construction Diagram Illustration # 62

Tools Needed for the Work

Bead Set Large and Small Illustration # 63

www.ingramcontent.com/pod-product-compliance
Lightning Source LLC
Chambersburg PA
CBHW081356070526
44583CB00020B/2571